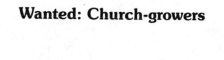

Wanted: Church-growers

WANTED CHURCH GROWERS

JERRY VINES

BROADMAN PRESS
NASHVILLE, TENNESSEE

ISBN: 0-8054-3008-3
Dewey Decimal Classification: 226.6
Subject Heading: BIBLE. N.T. ACTS // CHURCH
Library of Congress Card Catalog Number: 90-31925

Printed in the United States of America

Unless otherwise stated, all Scripture quotations are from the King James Version of the Bible.

Library of Congress Cataloging-in-Publication Data

Vines, Jerry.
    Wanted : church growers / Jerry Vines.
      p.   cm.
    Sequel to: Wanted : soul-winners.
    ISBN 0-8054-3008-3
    1. Church growth—Sermons. 2. Bible. N.T. Acts—Sermons.
  3. Sermons, American. 4. Baptists—Sermons. I. Title.
    BV652.25.V56 1990
254'.5—dc20   90-31925
                                                   CIP

To Clarence and Ruby Vines,
my Christian parents,
Who have loved and supported me
Throughout my life and ministry.

Contents

1
The Power of Pentecost

The Holy Ghost is here,
Where saints in prayer agree,
As Jesus' parting Gift is near
Each pleading company.
     —Charles Haddon Spurgeon

Acts 2:1-36

And when the day of Pentecost was fully come, they were all with one accord in one place.

And suddenly there came a sound from heaven as of a rushing mighty wind, and it filled all the house where they were sitting.

And there appeared unto them cloven tongues like as of fire, and it sat upon each of them.

And they were all filled with the Holy Ghost, and began to speak with other tongues, as the Spirit gave them utterance.

And there were dwelling at Jerusalem Jews, devout men, out of every nation under heaven.

Now when this was noised abroad, the multitude came together, and were confounded, because that every man heard them speak in his own language.

And they were all amazed and marveled, saying one to another, Behold, are not all these which speak Galilaeans?

And how hear we every man in our own tongue, wherein we were born?

Parthians, and Medes, and Elamites, and the dwellers in Mesopotamia, and in Judea, and Cappadocia, in Pontus, and Asia,

Phrygia, and Pamphylia, in Egypt, and in the parts of Libya about Cyrene, and strangers of Rome, Jews and proselytes,

Cretes and Arabians, we do hear them speak in our tongues the wonderful works of God.

And they were all amazed, and were in doubt, saying one to another, What meaneth this?

Others mocking said, These men are full of new wine.

But Peter, standing up with the eleven, lifted up his voice, and said unto them, Ye men of Judea, and all *ye* that dwell at Jerusalem, be this known unto you, and hearken to my words:

For these are not drunken, as ye suppose, seeing it is *but* the third hour of the day.

But this is that which was spoken by the prophet Joel;

And it shall come to pass in the last days, saith God, I will pour out of my Spirit upon all flesh: and your sons and your daughters shall prophesy, and your young men shall see visions, and your old men shall dream dreams:

And on my servants and on my handmaidens I will pour out in those days of my Spirit; and they shall prophesy:

And I will show wonders in heaven above, and signs in the earth beneath; blood, and fire, and vapor of smoke:

The sun shall be turned into darkness, and the moon into blood, before that great and notable day of the Lord come:

And it shall come to pass, *that* whosoever shall call on the name of the Lord shall be saved.

Ye men of Israel, hear these words; Jesus of Nazareth, a man approved of God among you by miracles and wonders and signs, which God did by him in the midst of you, as ye yourselves also know:

Him, being delivered by the determinate counsel and foreknowledge of God, ye have taken, and by wicked hands have crucified and slain:

Whom God hath raised up, having loosed the pains of death: because it was not possible that he should be held of it.

For David speaketh concerning him, I foresaw the Lord always before my face, for he is on my right hand, that I should not be moved:

Therefore did my heart rejoice, and my tongue was glad; moreover also my flesh shall rest in hope:

Because thou wilt not leave my soul in hell, neither wilt thou suffer thine Holy One to see corruption.

Thou hast made known to me the ways of life; thou shalt make me full of joy with thy countenance.

Men *and* brethren, let me freely speak unto you of the patriarch David, that he is both dead and buried, and his sepulcher is with us unto this day.

Therefore being a prophet, and knowing that God had sworn with an oath to him, that of the fruit of his loins, according to the flesh, he would raise up Christ to sit on his throne;

He seeing this before spake of the resurrection of Christ, that his soul was not left in hell, neither his flesh did see corruption.

This Jesus hath God raised up, whereof we all are witnesses.

Therefore being by the right hand of God exalted, and having received of the Father the promise of the Holy Ghost, he hath shed forth this, which ye now see and hear.

For David is not ascended into the heavens: but he saith him-

self, The LORD said unto my Lord, Sit thou on my right hand,
Until I make thy foes thy footstool.

Therefore let all the house of Israel know assuredly, that God
hath made that same Jesus, whom ye have crucified, both Lord
and Christ.

Certain groups claim to have a corner on the power of the Holy Spirit. They often refer to themselves as "full gospel" people, and they seem to emphasize the Day of Pentecost almost to the exclusion of all else. I believe the power of Pentecost is for every blood-bought, born-again believer.

There is widespread confusion about the genuine significance of the Day of Pentecost—and also subsequent encounters with the Holy Spirit in the Book of Acts. We must recover the spiritual power that was unleashed in the lives of the New Testament church.

One time a young preacher was sharing the fact that we need "it," "it" being the Holy Spirit. As many have mistakenly done, the preacher referred to the Holy Spirit as "it." An older preacher answered, "He's not it. He's He—a person."

Perhaps facetiously another fellow at the meeting remarked, "I don't care what you call Him, as long as we have Him, and He has us." We need it—the power and plentitude of the Holy Spirit.

Acts has often been called "The Acts of the Apostles," since they were the key instruments of God in the spreading of the gospel through the ministry of the early church. That term is somewhat appropriate. More than all else, I concur with the idea that Acts is "The Acts of the Holy Spirit." The early church could do nothing without the infilling, empowering, and leading of the Spirit, the third Person of the Godhead.

> And they were all amazed, and were in doubt, saying one to another, What meaneth this? (v. 12).

Whenever the power of God falls, this is the reaction in one form or another—doubt and questioning, amazement and astonishment. People are stirred deeply to ask probing questions about the supernatural workings of the Spirit.

The stage was set, and Peter delivered the message as the spokesman of the apostles: "But Peter, standing up with the eleven, lifted up his voice, and said unto them . . ." (v. 14a).

As Peter moved toward the close of his convicting message, his accusation stung the multitude:

> Therefore let all the house of Israel know assuredly, that God hath made that same Jesus, whom ye have crucified, both Lord and Christ (v. 36).

The good news of Christ, coupled with the bad for those who fail to repent, can pierce right down into human hearts.

> Now when they heard this, they were pricked in their heart, and said unto Peter and to the rest of the apostles, Men and brethren, what shall we do? (v. 37).

Peter answered immediately:

> Repent, and be baptized every one of you in the name of Jesus Christ for the remission of sins, and ye shall receive the gift of the Holy Ghost (v. 38).

Many in the crowd cried out about their predicament. Today many are blasé and unconcerned about the call of Christ. Instead of asking what they should do, they often ignore the message as though it does not relate to them, asking, if anything, "What's that got to do with me anyhow?"

Years ago I heard that the "average church" and the "average Christian" are bogged down somewhere between Calvary and Pentecost. They have been to Calvary for *pardon* but not to Pentecost for *power*. Bethlehem equals God with us. Calvary means God for us, but Pentecost vividly indicates: God in us to empower and motivate us to serve the Lord Jesus.

The brilliant J. B. Phillips once noted that modern churches are so fat and out of shape through prosperity. On the other hand, they are sometimes muscle-bound through over-organization. We urgently must have the wind and flame of Pentecost. Through God, the church must reharness the power.

The apostolic church was in dreadful need of power. Unlike many comfortable Christians today, their lives were on the line. Owning the name as a follower of "The Way" and later as a Christian was signing a death warrant. That is true in many nations today, where the leaders have outlawed Christianity, and preaching Christ is punishable by prison and/or death. Hundreds of our overseas missionaries live in constant tension and jeopardy.

This is the day of Pentecostal substitutes. We endeavor to wire ourselves with our own pyrotechnics and fireworks. We are like auxiliary power supplies—battery operated. We scramble around in an effort to manufacture our own power. There is nothing wrong with programs, pep, and promotions, *if* they are for the purpose of glorifying the Lord—but often we make subtle attempts to duplicate the power of the Spirit. We create a mini-storm from our wind and stoke our own fire. We are left bereft and hungry for the power of Pentecost.

We are so worried about getting out on a limb that we never even climb a tree. We are often terrified of "excesses" in relation to the ministry of the Holy Spirit. We are so afraid of "wildfire" that we end up having virtually no fire at all. What a tragedy that we fail to appropriate the power that is always available to every believer who will yield himself to the sway of the Spirit.

A mere reading of Holy-Spirit-centered scriptures may well revive the Christian who is weak and low on faith.

> And ye shall know that I *am* in the midst of Israel, and *that I am* the LORD your God, and none else: and my people shall never be ashamed.
>
> And it shall come to pass afterward, *that* I will pour out my spirit upon all flesh; and your sons and your daughters shall prophesy, your old man shall dream dreams, your young men shall see visions: (Joel 2:27-28).
>
> And, behold, I send the promise of my Father upon you: but tarry ye in the city of Jerusalem, until ye be endued with power from on high (Luke 24:49).
>
> And I will pray the Father, and he shall give you another Comforter, that he may abide with you forever;
>
> *Even* the Spirit of truth; whom the world cannot receive, because it seeth him not, neither knoweth him: but ye know him; for he dwelleth with you, and shall be in you.

I will not leave you comfortless: I will come to you (John 14:16-18).

But the Comforter, *which is* the Holy Ghost, whom the Father will send in my name, he shall teach you all things, and bring all things to your remembrance, whatsoever I have said unto you (John 15:26).

Nevertheless I tell you the truth; It is expedient for you that I go away: for if I go not away, the Comforter will not come unto you; but if I depart, I will send him unto you.

And when he is come, he will reprove the world of sin, and of righteousness, and of judgment:

Of sin, because they believe not on me;

Of righteousness, because I go to my Father, and ye see me no more;

Of judgment, because the prince of this world is judged.

I have yet many things to say unto you, but ye cannot bear them now.

Howbeit when he, the Spirit of truth, is come, he will guide you into all truth: for he shall not speak of himself; but whatsoever he shall hear, *that* shall he speak: and he will show you things to come.

He shall glorify me: for he shall receive of mine, and shall show *it* unto you.

All things that the Father hath are mine: therefore said I, that he shall take of mine, and shall show *it* unto you (John 16:7-15).

But ye shall receive power, after that the Holy Ghost is come upon you: and ye shall be witnesses unto me both in Jerusalem, and in all Judea, and in Samaria, and unto the uttermost part of the earth (Acts 1:8).

And when they had prayed, the place was shaken where they were assembled together; and they were all filled with the

Holy Ghost, and they spake the word of God with boldness
(Acts 4:31).

And grieve not the Holy Spirit of God, whereby ye are sealed
unto the day of redemption (Eph. 4:30).

Until Jesus returns in His second coming, believers will continue to debate the meaning of the events on the Day of Pentecost. Certain groups declare, "The initial evidence of the Holy
Ghost in one's life is speaking in tongues." Some claim that the
exact manifestations of Acts 2 can occur repeatedly. In connection with this subject is also the debate over gifts of the Spirit and
the fruit of the Spirit.

Joel clearly prophesied the coming of the Holy Spirit. The
promise was literally fulfilled on the Day of Pentecost. The outpouring of the Spirit was an historic fact. There is a sense in
which Pentecost will never be repeated. Before Pentecost the
Holy Spirit would enter a person's life for a specific purpose and
then depart. Later, He might return. This is borne out throughout
the Old Testament.

What was the difference between Pentecost and before? The
Holy Spirit at Pentecost and later would permanently indwell the
Christian—never to leave and never to forsake. Jesus promised
His disciples:

And I will pray the Father, and he shall give you another Comforter, that he may abide with you for ever (John 14:16).

First and foremost, Pentecost meant that the Holy Spirit would
permanently live within Christians. Secondly, the power is
always operative in the life of any born-again believer who lets
the Spirit control his heart, mind, soul, and body.

The Meaning of Pentecost

And when the day of Pentecost was come, they were all with one accord in one place (v. 1).

The reference here speaks of both divine and human *preparation*. In the Old Testament, God had sent down fire on various occasions. After Elijah prepared the sacrifice on Mount Carmel in the presence of the priests of Baal, God answered by fire, consuming the sacrifice, even the water in the trench around the altar. If Elijah had not obeyed God's instructions, the fire would not have fallen.

I am aware this fact is not original. Probably thousands of preachers and teachers have emphasized that the apostles and other disciples—120 in all—were in one accord and in one place. They were bound together in physical proximity but also in spiritual preparation. They were operating as though they were one. Their togetherness in Christ almost reminds us of a wedding ceremony. They were one in intent, purpose, and all concerns.

That is one of the beautiful aspects of brotherhood and sisterhood in Christ—from "every kindred, every tribe." Glenn Morris was a missionary to the Philippines when the Japanese invaded the islands in 1941. He was walking down a road when a column of Japanese troops approached. Morris prayed with all his heart, feeling that they might either capture him or kill him.

A Japanese captain stepped down from his vehicle and asked Morris, "Are you a Christian?" to which the missionary replied, "Oh, yes, I am a Christian. I am a follower of the Lord Jesus Christ!"

The captain, a military man from a hostile nation, politely bowed, then stepped forward to offer Morris his hand. The light of heaven was upon the captain's face as he testified, "I, too, am a Christian!" He shook hands with the missionary and then rejoined his troops.

"In Christ there is no East or West, no North or South." We are one in spirit under the blood-stained banner of our Lord and Savior. There is no room for prejudice or animosity. Our Lord has broken down the middle wall of partition between us (see Eph. 2:14).

Christians are diversified—"red and yellow, black and white." When they are one in the Spirit, mountains of spiritual obstacles are moved.

Consider the diversity of the apostles. Peter was brash and impetuous, sometimes downright obnoxious. John was more meditative and reflective, even though we have ample reasons to believe that he and his brother, James, were at times prideful and hot-headed. They were called Boanerges, "the sons of thunder," not only because of their father but also because they had a tendency to blow up. All of the others had their own peculiarities. Some of the apostles were introverted and withdrawn. Others were outspoken. But in Christ there can be unity amid diversity.

On the Day of Pentecost these multifaceted people were fused together because of the Holy Spirit—one in thought, one in purpose, one in spiritual truth. They were woven together into the tapestry of God's love. We have a union with God that automatically links us with every Christian on the face of the earth. Those disciples were rooted and grounded in their Master.

The greatest cohesive factor is when a group of believers—a church—becomes caught up, in one accord, in obeying the command of Christ to fan out into the community to reach people for Him.

Paul often commended the churches he had founded. He would first compliment them, and he usually found the good. Then, if he had to, he "lowered the boom." God should always receive the glory, yet there are times when the people of God ought to be commended. The reason our church, or any church, can continue to reach people is because the members commit themselves to witness. Even though our church is in the inner city, we have remained there and continued to baptize hundreds a year, because hundreds of our members are soul-winners. Any church which consistently reaches men and women, boys and girls must lay aside its differences and peculiarities and come to-gether for our number-one purpose—being church-builders for Jesus.

They were "in one place." The upper room was pre-cisely where God wanted them to be. Being where God wants you to be is absolutely vital. I think of Gideon with a small band of 300 men. They conquered the Midianite army of thou-sands. How did they? One primary reason is discovered in Judges 7:21:

> And they stood every man in his place round about the camp:
> and all the host [Midianites] ran, and cried, and fled (Jud. 7:21).

There is a statement fraught with meaning. "They stood every man in his place round about the camp." Those men were in their expected, appointed places, as were the 120 in the Upper Room.

If Gideon and his men, and if the apostles and other disciples, had responded as we often do today, I can imagine the alibis: "Andrew won't be here because he's down at the beach. He sent his regards. He says he's with us in spirit."

"John got his feelings hurt in Bible study. Oh, he'll eventually be back, I think."

"Matthew isn't present. His Aunt Hepzibah came to visit, so he'll have to stay home with his company."

"Man, this fellow Gideon is exacting. He wants me to stand in my station, and it's so uncomfortable in this heat. I'll fake sickness."

Ridiculous, isn't it? Yet, we hear this kind of rationalization all the time. If the 120 Christians in the Upper Room had exhibited that sort of lackadaisical attitude, there never would have been the prayer meeting which prepared them for the coming of the Holy Spirit. They prayed for the Spirit to come down. I heard years ago: "We try to *work up* the power of the Holy Spirit. That won't work. We have to *pray down* the power."

Those Christians were prepared and also available. Years ago a major-league pitcher, whose first name slips my mind, was called "Available" Jones. He was ready to step onto the mound whenever he was called. Highly successful for a relief pitcher, he rose to the occasion when it seemed defeat was in sight. If only we could be "available" Christians. The highest honor you can receive is simply to be available to Jesus—to do His bidding, to stand by for Him. A. C. Palmer wrote:

> Ready to speak, ready to warn,
> Ready o'er souls to yearn;
> Ready in life, ready in death
> Ready for His return.
>
> Ready to go, ready to stay;
> Ready my place to fill;
> Ready for service, lowly or great;
> Ready to do His will.

Yield yourself to the leading of the Holy Spirit, and God will miraculously work through and in you. Like those Upper-Room Christians, make sure to be in the right place at the right time doing the right thing.

We have dealt with human preparation. Now we touch on the divine. Pentecost was fifty days after the Passover. The Hebrews highly regarded Pentecost, in addition to the Passover. Christ was crucified on Friday of Passover week.

As Jesus was with His apostles on Mount Olivet, and about to ascend to the Father, He instructed them:

> . . . wait for the promise of the Father, which, saith he, ye have heard of me. For John truly baptized with water; but ye shall be baptized with the Holy Ghost not many days hence (Acts 1:4*b*-5).

The Lord had repeatedly promised the outpouring of the Holy Spirit. Here He referred to the baptism of the Holy Spirit. The Holy Spirit was coming to occupy His new Temple, His new Tabernacle—those who would receive Christ as Lord and Savior. In the Old Testament, God had filled the Holy of Holies with the Shekinah glory from heaven which had penetrated the inmost part of the Tabernacle and later the Temple. Through divine intervention, the prophecy was fulfilled.

In the comforting fourteenth chapter of John, Jesus reassured the apostles about the ministry and purpose of the Spirit.

> And I will pray the Father, and he shall give you another comforter, that he may abide with you for ever; Even the Spirit of truth: whom the world cannot receive, because it seeth him not, neither knoweth him: but ye know him: but ye know him: for he dwelleth with you, and shall be in you (vv. 16-17).

What difference did the coming of the Holy Spirit make? The Holy Spirit would no longer be a temporary guest. He would baptize Jesus' disciples into the body of Christ. Every believer is baptized into the body of Christ and is indwelt by the Spirit *forever*. This knowledge can change one's whole outlook and perspective.

Now let's look at . . .

The Miracles of Pentecost

> And suddenly there came a sound from heaven as of a rushing mighty wind, and it filled all the house where they were sitting (v. 2).

There were two miracles manifested—sound and sight. "There came a sound from heaven as of a rushing mighty wind, and it filled all the house where they were sitting." The place where they had been praying for ten days was filled with the sound. The Greek word for breath was used in this verse. It was equivalent to the Old Testament word for breath, which was often translated "soul." The breath of the Holy Spirit is the breath of God.

The wind became a symbol of the Holy Spirit. The wind is invisible. So is the Holy Spirit. Jesus unveiled this mystery to Nicodemus.

> The wind blows where it wishes and you hear the sound of it, but do not know where it comes from and where it is going: so is everyone who is born of the Spirit (John 3:8, NASB).

The "natural man" without Christ will put no stock in the invisible realities of God. Consider Paul's comment about the unbelievers who make light of the "invisible" truths of the supernatural world.

For since the creation of the world His invisible attributes, His eternal power and divine nature, have been clearly seen, being understood through what has been made, so that they are without excuse (Rom. 1:20, NASB).

The lost world is not going to believe without seeing.

There are realities not visible to the naked eye. The Spirit is like the wind—invisible—yet the impact of the wind is felt. Even a tornado itself is not seen. The visible funnel consists of debris and materials sucked up by the velocity of the wind. The Spirit enters a life as the wind of God.

The wind is also *irresistible*. No one can stop it. Neither can one buy three gallons of wind. You can recognize when the wind of heaven has blown across a person's life or a church's witness. I recall when Hurricane Frederick struck Mobile where I was pastoring at the time. At the height of the hurricane, our minister of music became concerned about the gate on his fence outside. He crawled into the yard and tied down the gate. In the morning the whole fence, along with the gate, was gone. Wind can effect change, not only in nature but most certainly in human nature.

The wind is also *indispensable*. Without the wind with its effects, life could become unbearable. The wind can cool the environment. Warm breezes can also dispel the cold. It also assists in the process of fertilization of plant life. In the spiritual life, the wind of the Holy Spirit energizes the church. In the case of Ezekiel and the valley of dry bones, the body was still dead, even after the bones came together. There was no life until God breathed on those reconstructed bones (see Ezek. 37).

God breathed life into that body. The breath of God empowers the body of Christ. We are wasting our time unless the Wind of God blows.

Then there was the miracle of *sight*.

And there appeared unto them cloven tongues like as of fire,
and they sat upon each of them (v. 2).

As verse 4 indicates, "And they were all filled with the Holy
Ghost . . ." They then spoke God's message in "other tongues."
Why? So they could make a show? So they could boast about
having supernatural power? So they could talk of "the initial evidence of the Holy Ghost"? No, God intended that all those nations and ethnic groups hear the gospel and understand it in their
own language. I contend that the initial evidence of the Holy
Ghost is sharing the Word of God.

"As of fire . . ." What a suggestive symbol. Fire cleanses, clear-
ing away the dross and waste materials. The Holy Spirit serves as
a purifying agent in the lives of God's children. When the Holy
Spirit is honored the people of God will become cleaner and
purer. Fire consumes. It burns up self-righteousness and sins
both of the flesh and the human spirit. Fire creates fire, and there
is a resultant chain reaction of holiness and purity as the flames of
God sweep through a community of Christians.

Negativism often strangles the churches of the Lord Jesus.
One Christian on fire, though, will spiritually ignite other Christians. It is contagious. My first book was entitled *Fire in the Pulpit.*
Yes, indeed, the man in the pulpit ought to set the example and
fan the flames of passion for souls.

Are you filled with the Holy Spirit? The filling of the Holy Spirit
is not for a select few. When we were born again, regenerated,
we were baptized in the Spirit. There is one baptism, but many
fillings. Only a short time after the Day of Pentecost, the believers
were again filled with the Spirit:

> And when they had prayed, the place was shaken where they were assembled together: and they were all filled with the Holy Ghost, and they spake the word of God with boldness (Acts 4:31).

The filling of the Spirit is the norm for every disciple of Christ. How can we do anything worthwhile without the filling of the Spirit? What does being filled imply? It means you are under the control and dominion of the Spirit—that you are absolutely permeated with the Spirit's influence and under the conscious leading of the Spirit.

The Holy Spirit will enable you to witness. A primary reason most church members will not witness is fear, according to the late Roland Q. Leavell. I am a timid person. Most people may not believe that. Maybe at times I have more facility to preach to large crowds than to meet a person heart to heart and eyeball to eyeball. When I was a teenager I was petrified about witnessing, but I did. I remembered the reassurance of Jesus. "It is not you that speaketh, but the Spirit from the Father." Regardless of the barriers, God can use you and me as witnesses.

Then there was . . .

The Message of Pentecost

> But Peter, standing up with the eleven, lifted up his voice, and said unto them, Ye men of Judea, and all ye that dwell at Jerusalem, be this known unto you, and hearken to my words (Acts 2:14).

Before Peter preached, the disciples were preaching and bearing witness. When the day started they were sitting. Now they were standing and courageously proclaiming Christ. Peter, who had betrayed his Lord and slinked off into the darkness, was now a firebrand for the crucified, buried, risen, ascended, and returning Lord. In his message he ran the gamut on the keyboard of the gospel.

Every God-anointed preacher should key in on his themes:

1. He Declared Jesus, His Death and Resurrection: . . . (Acts 2:22-24).
2. He Quoted David Concerning Jesus: . . . (Acts 2:25-28).
3. From David's Statement Peter Argued as Follows [concerning the announcement by David of Jesus' Resurrection]: . . . (Acts 2:29-31).
4. Living Witnesses of the Resurrection Presented: "This Jesus did God raise, whereof we all are witnesses" (Acts 2:3).
5. The Exaltation Established by the Descent of the Holy Spirit: . . . (Acts 2:33).
6. The Exaltation Proved by David . . . (Acts 2:34,35).
7. Peter's Fervent Exhortation: . . . (Acts 2:36).
8. Convinced and Convicted People Asked a Serious Question: . . . (Acts 2:37).
9. The Holy Spirit Gave the Answer Through Peter: . . . (Acts 2:38,39).
10. Peter Urged Decision: . . . (Acts 2:40).[1]

The power of God's Spirit will energize you and activate you. On the Day of Pentecost, the disciples witnessed in the streets before Peter preached. The witnessing of Christians will always lend credibility to the preaching from the pulpit.

Pentecostal Christianity entails preaching and witnessing in the power of the Living Christ. It means preaching the whole counsel of God. The "old, old story" never becomes old.

This kind of preaching will lead to the question, "Brethren, what shall we do?" And the answer will be plain, "Repent and be baptized." "Believe on the Lord Jesus Christ, and thou shalt be saved and thy house" (Acts 16:31).

> Breathe on me, Breath of God,
> Till I am wholly Thine,
> Till all this earthly part of me
> Glows with Thy fire divine.
> —Edwin Hatch

Note

1. "Pentecost, in New Testament," *Holman Master Study Bible* (Nashville: Holman Bible Publishers, 1983), 1695.

2
Just A Prayer Meeting

Prayer is the most powerful form of energy one can generate. The influence of prayer on the human mind and body are as demonstrable as that of the secreting glands. It supplies us with a flow of sustaining power in our daily lives.

—Alexis Carrel

Acts 4:23-31

And being let go, that is Peter and John, they went to their own company and reported all that the chief priests and elders had said unto them. And when they heard that, they lifted up their voice to God with one accord, and said, Lord, thou art God, which hast made heaven, and earth, and the sea, and all that in them is: Who by the mouth of thy servant David has said, Why did the heathen rage, and the people imagine vain things? The kings of the earth stood up, and the rulers were gathered together against the Lord, and against his Christ. For of the truth against thy holy child Jesus, whom thou hast anointed, both Herod, and Pontius Pilate, with the Gentiles, and the people of Israel, were gathered together, For to do whatsoever thy hand and thy counsel determined before to be done. And now, Lord, behold their threatenings: and grant unto thy servants, that

with all boldness they may speak thy word, By stretching forth
thine hand to heal; and that signs and wonders may be done by
the name of thy holy child Jesus. And when they had prayed,
the place was shaken where they were assembled together; and
they were all filled with the Holy Ghost, and they spake the word
of God with boldness.

It was only a prayer meeting, and yet what occurred there has been and will be commemorated for all eternity on the pages of the Holy Scriptures. Only a prayer meeting, but it shook them, and the truths shake us right now.

Peter and John had been dismissed by the Sanhedrin. They had spent the night in jail; they had gone before the Sanhedrin which had commanded them never again to speak in the name of Jesus. Peter and John said, "Whether it be good to hearken unto men rather than unto God, you be the judge. We cannot but speak the things which we have seen and heard." After that threat and their statement, they were released, and the Bible says they went to a prayer meeting.

It was just a prayer meeting, but it was an altogether different atmosphere for these apostles. They moved from a meeting of *peril* into a meeting of *prayer*, from an atmosphere where they were surrounded by threatening, ridicule, and insult, into a place where they were engulfed with love, fellowship, and understanding. It was only a prayer meeting, but, oh, what a difference that change in atmosphere made for them!

It is the desire of every genuine Bible-believing church to have the power which the churches in the first century had. We will not have the power they had until we learn to pray like they prayed. There is power in prayer. It was only a prayer meeting, but, oh, the power that was unleashed on the city of Jerusalem as a result of that gathering for prayer!

Every time of opposition is an opportunity for prayer. Every challenge is an opportunity to come to God in prayer. We meet our enemies with prayer. We solve our problems with prayer.

This world looks on the prayer meetings of believers, and they feel that nothing of significance is going on. Yes, only a prayer meeting but the God of heaven is interested, and the God of heaven looks on and answers when people pray.

Melanchthon in the Reformation said, "Trouble and perplexity drive me to prayer, but prayer drives perplexity and trouble away from me." When you and I learn the power of prayer, it makes the difference. *Only a prayer meeting.*

Only a little widow on her knees in that small apartment, and yet as she prays, she lays hold of the very power sources that move this universe. Only a little man in an isolated place somewhere, faithfully laboring and serving the Lord. Only a prayer meeting when he kneels to pray, and yet the angels of heaven hold their breath to see what God is going to do in that man's life in response to prayer.

I am convinced that the great powerhouse of every church is God's people gathering together for corporate or for private prayer.

There's an animal in Africa known as the gnu. It is a rather unusual animal. When an enemy approaches that animal, it falls to its knees, and it literally leaps to attack from its knees. You and I must meet every need on our knees. We must meet every opposition on our knees. We must encounter every enemy of the gospel on our knees. Only a prayer meeting, and yet who knows what God may do when people gather together for prayer? Oh, what a privilege it is to pray! "Oh, what needless pain we bear, all because we do not carry everything to God in prayer." Only a prayer meeting, but let's look at it together.

I call your attention first of all to . . .

The People of This Prayer Meeting

"And being let go" [that is Peter and John, released by the Sanhedrin] "they went to their own company . . ." That little phrase speaks volumes about Peter and John. When they were released, they immediately headed for their own company. That was normal. People have a tendency to go where they naturally feel at home. They went to a prayer meeting. Vance Havner used to ask, "Where do you go when you're let go?" "And being let go, they went to their own company."

There is a law which is known as the law of affinity, and it means that likes attract. This is true, for instance, in the physical realm. Particles of matter attract one another; they have an affinity for one another. This is also true in the social realm. Do you remember hearing your mama say, when you were an adolescent, "Remember now, Son; remember, Susie, birds of a feather flock together"? That is exactly true. People who have common interests get together. There is *intellectual* affinity. Those who are in particular professions have a bent to form societies and gather together. Those who are interested in similar *political* enterprises have a tendency to get together.

There is also *spiritual* affinity. In other words, if you love the Lord Jesus Christ, then you want to be around those who love Him too. If you love the concerns of God, you want to be where they are. If you enjoy reading and studying the Bible, you want to be where those practices are going on.

Say, where do *you* go when you're let go? Where do you go when you're on vacation? I mean, do you go to your own company? Are you attracted to those who are of like mind and heart? What you are will help determine what you do. It's sad, isn't it, that some Christians compromise their testimony when they're on vacation? And isn't it a heartache to the loving heart of our eternal God that there are those who, when they're off at a resort somewhere, or when they're aboard a luxury liner, compromise their convictions and their testimonies? What do you do when you're away from home?

I remember in high school when we went on our senior trip. Classmates I had respected and looked up to "let it all hang out." I lost all my respect for some kids on that senior-high trip. Some of them drank I'd never seen drink before. They read magazines I'd never seen them read before. They gave up their convictions, and their standards were lowered.

Let me encourage you to be faithful to Christ. It was the *normal* thing for them to do—to go to the prayer meeting. It was also *needful* for them to do. Those two disciples, Peter and John, had a need to be in an atmosphere where there was some friendliness and acceptance. They had been in hostile territory. I mean, for several hours, all they believed had been attacked. Their faith had been shaken to its very foundation. They needed to be in an atmosphere of love and acceptance.

Many of you have a real battle on your job. You may be the only Christian, and you may encounter a constant barrage of ridicule with people making fun of your faith and your church. Isn't it wonderful to walk out of that atmosphere and to come into your place of worship on Sunday and at other times and be with your own company? It's wonderful, isn't it? Many of our members come to our services Sunday, Wednesday, and at other times when they are tired, burdened, under tremendous pressure from work. Many of them have backbreaking schedules. You say, "Preacher, why do they do that?" They're out there battling the world, the flesh, and the devil during the week, and they need the strength they derive from being among the people of God on a Wednesday night. We thank God for the crowd we have, but it ought to be jammed to the walls every Wednesday night. How can you go a solid week and not be in a place where there is prayer and singing the praises of Jesus and loving the Lord?

"And being let go, they went to their own company." The people of the meeting. It was only a prayer meeting, and yet Peter and John met the people of God there. Next we notice not only the people of the meeting, but also . . .

The Prayer of This Prayer Meeting

They came back and gave their report (v. 23). And so the report called for prayer. In verse 24 it says, "And when they heard that" [that is, they heard what had taken place] "they lifted up their voice to God with one accord, . . ." Now notice this: *they* lifted up *their*—plural—voice—singular—to God with one accord. Now that seems to indicate that there is one person who voiced the prayer, but in so doing that person was expressing the prayer of all the congregation. Somehow the Lord led one man to pray what everybody wanted to pray at that particular time.

That's very often true, isn't it? When I hear somebody praying, I say, "Amen, Lord. That's what I'd be praying if I were praying out loud."

This was a prayer meeting, and they began to pray with one accord. What a wonderful experience this is! If you want a blessing sometime, let me encourage you to study the prayers of the Bible. Let's look at this prayer. Here I learn about the blessing of prayer. Those people were a little speck on the globe; only a little group of people. Just a little prayer meeting, and yet they were addressing the very God of this universe. That is one of the most astounding truths in all of life. Through the medium of prayer you have access to the God who created everything your eyes can see and the things your eyes cannot see. By prayer you have the opportunity to walk into the very throne room of the God of this universe. What a privilege!

A few years ago, I was sent an invitation to attend the president's prayer breakfast. I was not able to go, but I was really honored to think, *Boy, I might be able to go up there and pray with the president!* And I have a feeling that if you got a letter in the morning, "Dear Mr. So and So, President Bush gives his personal invitation to you to attend his prayer breakfast next Monday morning at the White House," you'd say to your wife, "Listen, we must go to the store and buy new clothes."

"Why?"

"Well, I'm going to pray with the president next Monday morning. He's asked me to come pray." You would make all the arrangements. At the job you'd walk in and brag, "Well, what are you all doing next Monday morning? Oh, you don't know what you're doing? Well, guess what I'm doing next Monday morning? Man, I am going to the White House! President Bush has invited me. I am going up to the White House, and he and I are going to pray together before breakfast."

I have something better than that, friend. I have good news for you. I am here to announce to you that, though you may feel like you're the smallest, most insignificant person on this globe, you may feel like you're the least of the least of the children of God, you have the wonderful privilege of talking to God Himself in prayer. You may attend a prayer meeting every morning with the Lord of this universe!

God has filled this Bible with promises to encourage you to talk with Him. "Ask and it shall be given unto you, seek and ye shall find, knock and it shall be opened unto you." God is calling. "Please talk with Me." Isn't it a tragedy that some may go for days and days and not pray?

I want you to notice not only the *blessing* of prayer but also the *basis* of prayer. They began to pray to the Lord God who made the heaven and the earth. Recognize how God-centered this prayer is. The prayer begins with the word *Lord*. "Lord, thou art God." The Greek word *kurios* actually means "ruler," even "despot." And it means one in absolute control. The prayer ends with the name *Jesus*. It is a God-centered prayer. Jesus gave the Model Prayer, and He said that when we pray, it ought to be: "Our Father which art in heaven . . ." How do you open your prayers? What do you do when you communicate in prayer? You must focus your attention on the Lord. Be God-centered.

You learn about God, first of all who God is—the God "who made heaven and earth and all that in them is." This God to whom we pray is the God who created everything. I do not believe that man is an accident. I do not believe that man is a "fortuitous concourse of atoms," that we just happened. I believe that mankind is the very apex, the very zenith of God's creative power. God formed man and "breathed into his nostrils the breath of life."

Notice Peter also learned not only who God is, but what God has to say. Verse 25: "Who by the mouth of thy servant David has said . . ." and then he quoted Psalm 2:1. These people made the Word of God a part of their prayer. Psalm 2:1 parallels exactly what occurred when Jesus was put on trial before Herod and Pontius Pilate.

They applied the Scriptures to their contemporary situation. What this says to me is that nothing ever comes into your life that takes God by surprise. God created you; God knew you before you were born—all about you.

When you apply the truth of the Bible to the circumstances of your life, it takes all of the uncertainty out of it. Remember, God is in control. In verse 28, he says, "For to do," talking about what Herod, Pontius Pilate, the Gentiles, and the people of Israel did, "For to do whatsoever," (talking to the Lord) ". . . thy hand and thy counsel determined before to be done." In other words, "God, you're in control."

"Oh God, this has happened to me," we cry. "Lord, Lord, what am I going to do? Lord, we can't handle this situation." But Jesus can. God is in charge and never forget it.

Now, the basis of prayer is in the Word of God. Notice in verse 29 their request, "And now, Lord, behold their threatenings." They just turned the problem over to the Lord. "Lord, there's the problem. Please tend to it. Look at their threatenings!"

I think about Hezekiah in the Old Testament. One time his enemies wrote him a deadly, threatening letter. So Hezekiah went into the house of the Lord and spread it out before the Lord as if to say, "Lord, would you look at what those enemies wrote? Lord, how about your taking care of this?" Well, that's exactly what they did with Peter and John's situation. They had been threatened never again to speak in the name of Jesus. They laid the problems before God in prayer: "Lord take care of those problems."

I remember the times I have not been able to sleep at night. When I can't, I start praying and usually I go to sleep soon after I start. One particular time I couldn't go to sleep, and I thought about "He that keepeth Israel shall neither slumber nor sleep." I suddenly thought, "Now, wait a minute, Lord. That verse says You don't ever sleep. Lord, that means, then, that whatever is keeping me awake, and whatever problems may be robbing me of sleep, Lord, You know about those problems, too. Lord, that verse says You neither slumber nor sleep. Lord, if both of us are awake, I think I'll just go on to sleep. Good night, Lord." Soon I was asleep.

Behold their threatenings! Turn your problems over to the Lord in prayer.

Oh, behold their threatenings! There was only one request in this entire prayer. They asked God for only one thing. Verse 29: ". . . and grant unto thy servants, that with all boldness they may speak thy word." They were simply praying to be able to do what they were commanded by the Sanhedrin not to do. "Lord, give us boldness; help us to keep on doing what we've been doing."

How can you be sure you can get your prayers answered? I want to give you a guarantee, a prayer you can pray that will always be answered by God. Now I can't always make this promise. Sometimes we pray prayers, and they're not answered. In one sense of the word they're all answered. God gives one of three answers to prayer, doesn't He? God will either answer yes, no, or wait a while. Aren't you ladies glad God didn't answer your prayer and you didn't marry that first guy you asked the Lord for? See? Aren't you pleased with that? Sometimes the Lord answers: "No, uh-uh, that's not good for you. I'm not going to give that to you." Then sometimes the Lord advises "wait." But here is the prayer that will always be answered. Find a commandment from the Word of God, something that God commands you to do. Do you follow me? Now that's what happened here. See, the Lord had commanded them to be witnesses. Before Jesus went back to heaven He gathered those disciples together, and he said, "Go, and make disciples of all nations beginning at Jerusalem and to the uttermost parts of the earth" (Acts 1:8). They were praying, "Lord, You give us boldness to do what You told us to do."

Latch onto a commandment from the Lord and then pray that to the Lord. I will guarantee you that the Lord will answer that prayer!

You can't miss it when you start praying for what God has told you to do. The Sanhedrin threatened, "Shut up, don't witness anymore."

"Lord, give us boldness. Help us to be more faithful to witness for you than we've ever been before," was the disciples's prayer.

Now, I want you to notice . . .

The Power of This Prayer Meeting

See verse 31: "And when they had prayed [only a prayer meeting . . . but look] the place was shaken where they were assembled together." Oh, I have a feeling that the Lord became so thrilled about what His people were doing down here. The Lord was lovingly rocking the cradle of the infant church. He shook that place.

Do you remember when Paul and Silas were in the Philippian jail and began to pray and sing praises to God. The Bible reports there was an earthquake. God is interested in praying people who want to do His will. And the building was shaken! Only a prayer meeting, but it shook a building. Only a prayer meeting, but it shook a group of disciples, shook a city for God, resulting in thousands of people being saved.

Now notice the *power*. Something happened to them. Look at it—"And they were all filled with the Holy Spirit" (see v. 31). They were all filled with the Holy Spirit.

There is no mention here that they spoke with tongues. People ask the question, "Preacher, what is the evidence of the filling of the Holy Spirit? Is it tongues?" No, not according to the Scriptures. "Is it power to do miracles?" No, that is not the Bible's evidence of the filling. If you will study the Book of Acts carefully, you will discover that the evidence of being filled with the Spirit is soul-winning power, power to be a witness for Jesus Christ. A witnessing Christian is a Spirit-filled Christian and vice versa. They were all filled with the Holy Spirit.

This was the third time they were filled with the Holy Spirit. On the Day of Pentecost they were all filled with the Holy Spirit. At the beginning of this chapter, Simon Peter was filled with the Holy Spirit before the Sanhedrin. They prayed, the building was shaken, and they were all filled with the Holy Spirit. Three times already in four chapters, they experienced a filling of the Holy Spirit.

Folks inquire, "Well, preacher, do you believe in the second blessing?" Yessiree, I believe in the second blessing. I believe in more than that. I believe in the third blessing and in the fifth blessing and the tenth blessing and the thousandth blessing! We daily need to be filled with the Spirit of God. There is one baptism, many fillings. Day by day we ought to claim the filling of the Holy Spirit.

Back where I came from you couldn't have revival except for one month of the year in August. The backsliders would get right, and it seemed you had to get saved and baptized in August because we wouldn't have another revival for a year. There was an old brother who always got stirred up in the meeting. So he came down one night with his dear little wife, and the old brother began to pray, "Oh, Lord, fill me. Oh, Lord, fill me. Lord, fill me." And the little wife was overheard to pray, "Don't do it, Lord. He leaks." We all leak from time to time.

The Bible knows nothing of an experience where you hit a certain level in your Christian life, and then you stay on that high plane, never deviating from it. Simon Peter one moment was as full of God as he could possibly be, and by divine revelation he confessed, "Thou art the Christ, the Son of the living God." And in an instant, he was rebuking the Lord Jesus, "Far be it from you, Lord. Don't let this come to you." Jesus retorted, "Get thee behind me, Satan." He went from the heights of filling to the depths of being used of the devil.

The truth of the matter is we need a constant infilling of spiritual power. And that's why you ought to begin every day in a little prayer meeting. You say, "Well, only a prayer meeting?" Yes, but in that little prayer meeting with which you begin your day you can claim the filling of God's power. They were all filled with the Holy Spirit.

God can do nothing through you until first of all He does something in you. You must yield the controls of your life. God's Spirit is in you if you're a born-again believer. You do not pray that you will get the Holy Spirit, but you do pray that the Holy Spirit will get you. He did something *to* them, and second, he did something *through* them. And they were able to speak the Word of God with boldness.

There it is. "What did they pray for, preacher?" Verse 29: ". . . grant unto thy servants, that with all boldness they may speak thy word." That's what they asked for, but what did they get? Verse 31: ". . . and they spake the word of God with boldness." "Lord, give us boldness." What did God give them? Boldness to speak the Word of God. God uses prayer to put power into the hearts of His people that people might be saved. Only a prayer meeting, and yet a building was shaken. Only a prayer meeting, and yet a little group of people were moved closer to God. Only a prayer meeting, and yet soul-winning power emanated. Only a prayer meeting, and yet Jerusalem was stirred, moved, and thrust closer to God. Only a prayer meeting—but who knows what God will do when a group of people begin to pray?

One church had bought a new organ and had invited a noted musician to play on the organ and have a dedication recital for the organ. The noted musician sat down at the organ, but as he touched the keys of the organ there was not a sound. The custodian was aware of the fact that he had not turned the organ on. Prayer was called for, and someone began to pray. And as they prayed, the custodian jotted down a note, slipped it into the hands of the organist, and here's what it said: "After the prayer, the power will come on." After the prayer, the power comes on. Only a prayer meeting, but it laid hold onto the very power of the God of this universe!

3
The Inner Life of the Church

Where are kings and empires now,
of old that went and came?
But, Lord, Thy church is praying yet,
a thousand years the same!
—Arthur Cleveland Cox

Acts 4:32-37

And the multitude of them that believed were of one heart and of one soul: neither said any of them that ought of the things which he possessed was his own; but they had all things common. And with great power gave the apostles witness of the resurrection of the Lord Jesus: and great grace was upon them all. Neither was there any among them that lacked: for as many as were possessors of lands or houses sold them, and brought the prices of the things that were sold, And laid them down at the apostles feet: and distribution was made unto every man according as he had need. And Joses, who by the apostles was surnamed Barnabas, (which is, being interpreted, The son of consolation) a Levite, and of the country of Cyprus, Having land, sold it, and brought the money, and laid it at the apostles' feet.

As you read through the Book of Acts there is a series of summary statements of the life, growth, and work of the early church. We find this at the conclusion of the second chapter, after the Day of Pentecost and the great ingathering of souls—3,000 people won to the Lord. Then we are told in the closing verses of that chapter about the condition of the church in its progress. You discover the same thing in the end of Chapter 4, and several times later. It's as if the Holy Spirit gives us a snapshot of the inner life of the early church.

Of course, what a church is on the outside is very important. We're always concerned about our image and the testimony we render to those on the outside. The effectiveness of the testimony and the witness of a church on the outside will be largely dependent upon the inner life, the depths of the spirituality found inside the hearts of the believers. It shows us beneath the veneer what the church really is on the inside.

It's important what people think about us, but it is more important what God knows about us.

There are two aspects I want us to look at. First of all, there is . . .

The Matter of the Total Church

You will notice in verse 32 it says, "And the multitude of them . . ." In other words, the total church. Here is a beautiful picture of harmony and unity of purpose. We are told in verse 32 that they were of one heart and of one soul. They were together.

A church can do a great many things if it is together. In Psalm 33:1 the Bible says, "Behold how good and how pleasant it is for brethren to dwell together in unity." Take a group of carnal Christians, and you couldn't build a chicken coop with that crowd. But take a group of people who are in love with the Lord, who don't care who gets the credit, who want to do nothing but win people to Christ and lift up the lovely name of Jesus Christ, and you can see a miracle work for God done on the earth.

The multitude, we are told, was of one heart and of one soul. Now we view the expressions of this unity in several directions. First of all, there was *unity of experience*. This was the multitude of them that believed.

There are several titles for Christians in the New Testament. The word "Christian" occurs only two times in the entire New Testament. That's the most common word used to identify the followers of Jesus in our day. There were other terms used more often. Sometimes they were called "those of the Way." Very often they were called "the family," "the brothers and the sisters in Christ." But one of the terms used to describe early Christians was "believers." There was a unity of experience. A church is to be made up of people who have a common experience of heart commitment to the Lord Jesus Christ. *Believers.*

Some even have suggested we ought to change what we refer to as believers or Christians today. Some think Christian is a little threadbare, and maybe it's lost some of its impact and meaning in our generation. I don't think the solution is to change the use of the word. I think a better solution is to put real meaning and vitality into the word Christian. It ought to mean something if you call yourself a Christian. There ought to be some dynamism in that term if you name the name of Christ. A Christian is a follower of Jesus Christ. I think it is splendid that Christians are sometimes called believers. They have a personal, saving experience with Jesus Christ on the basis of a heart belief.

"That if thou shalt confess with thy mouth the Lord Jesus, and shalt believe in thine heart that God hath raised him from the dead, thou shalt be saved" (Rom. 10:9). "For with the heart man believeth unto righteousness" (v. 10a). There is a difference between believing in your head and believing in your heart.

Sometimes when I'm witnessing to a person one on one, I describe it this way: I say to him, "When I came into your house tonight, I looked at your sofa, and I believed in my head that your sofa would hold me up. But suppose I don't sit down. Suppose I simply stand in the middle of the room the rest of the night. Does your sofa do me any good?" They invariably answer, "Well, no, it won't do you any good." And I say, "Well, what did I have to do?"

"Well, you had to sit down."

"That is exactly right," I replied. It is one thing to believe in your head the sofa will hold you up; it's another to believe in your heart it will hold you up.

I have a feeling that a large percentage of people believe in their heads that Jesus actually lived, that He was born of a virgin, that He lived a sinless life, that He died on the cross, that three days later He rose again from the dead, and that He went back to heaven. You probably have no problems believing that in your head. But have you believed it in your heart? You can believe all of those facts in your head, die in your sins, and never be saved. The Bible says you've got to believe in your heart—a commitment of your heart to the Lord Jesus Christ, a surrender of your life. Are you a believer? With a heart belief, have you committed your life to Jesus Christ? There are some folks, I'm afraid, who are going to miss heaven by eighteen inches. They have it in the head, but they've never received Christ in their hearts. If you have never opened up your heart and invited Jesus in, do it now. I am not talking about church membership. I'm talking about in your heart of hearts, saying to the Lord, "Lord, I know I'm a sinner. I know I deserve the wages of sin. I know that Jesus paid those wages at Calvary's cross, and with all of my heart I invite Him into my heart, and I commit my life to Him as my Savior and as my Lord." Instantaneously, right on the spot, the miracle of the new birth will be performed, and you will be a true believer in the Lord Jesus Christ.

That's the only prerequisite for church membership I can find in the New Testament. In Acts 8, where Philip had gone out into the desert, there was an Ethiopian. Philip preached Jesus to him. And the eunuch asked, "Well, here's water. What hinders me from being baptized?" And Philip said, "Well, you've got to go on a six-month training course, and then take a test, and if you pass the test, then we'll let you join our church." Is that what he instructed the eunuch? Does your version put it that way? No!

He said, "What doth hinder me from being baptized?" Philip said, "If thou believest with all thine heart, thou mayest" (see Acts 8:26-39).

I know there may be some situations on mission fields and in other circumstances where it may be wise for a church to have some kind of waiting period. I am simply pointing out that the Scriptural norm for baptism and fellowship with the believers is when people have had a common experience of faith in the Lord Jesus Christ.

To be a believer in Jesus implies that your life ought to be different. It means your lifestyle should be controlled by the Holy Spirit—your reading, your entertainment, your talk, your attitude, your habits. You've committed your life to Christ. You're not your own anymore. You belong to the Lord Jesus Christ. They were believers in the early church. There was a unity of experience.

And then rather interestingly there was a *unity of expression* in this fellowship. The Bible indicates that the believers in Jerusalem were having a difficult time making ends meet. Some of them were very poor. The text says that no one in the fellowship thought that any of their possessions remained their own, but they had "all things common" (v. 32). The word "common" comes from *koinonia* (fellowship, a shared life). They had all things in common. There was a oneness in expression. The Bible says that these believers took the things they had and brought them and laid them at the feet of the apostles (v. 34). Now this seems to have been confined to the church in Jerusalem. There is no record that the larger church, as the church expanded, continued this practice. There is not a mandate given in the Scriptures that believers are to do this. It seems to have been an altogether voluntary matter done in the principle of love, not in the principle of law.

But there is a spiritual principle here that is applicable to believers in all churches in all generations.

The Matter of the Sacrificial Church

It is the principle of sacrifice on the parts of believers to do God's business in the church where they serve.

We are a tithing congregation at First Baptist Church, Jacksonville. We may have the largest number of tithers in our nation. I do not know. In fact, one of the most exciting times of the year is when we have our stewardship emphasis. There was a time when I preached on giving and was rather apologetic about it. And then it dawned on me that one of the greatest things in the world I could do for a Christian was to teach him to give God a minimum of 10 percent of his income. Don't argue, "Well, I'm not mature enough to be a tither. I'm just going to start giving a little bit; and if that makes me feel good, I'm going to start giving a little bit more." Since when do we have to bypass obeying what God says to do in His Word? If you wait around until you are mature enough to give 10 percent, you are never going to give it. Did you know that?

I hear people say, "Oh, if I had a million dollars, I'd really give a lot to my church." I rather doubt it. I don't think they would. If you're not faithful to God with what you have now, you're not going to tithe if you have a million dollars. You'd be stingier then than you are now. The tendency of money is to make one stingier.

This Scripture makes it plain that there ought to be a sacrificial spirit in the matter of your giving.

You say, "Preacher, the tithe is Old Testament. We're in the

New Testament." That's right. In the Old Testament they gave 10 percent or more. You don't like the Old Testament manner? Well, in the New Testament they gave 100 percent. Take your pick; it doesn't matter to me.

Percentages are totally beside the point. When a person loves the Lord and knows he belongs to Jesus, that love causes him to obey whatever Jesus says to do in the matter of your material means. Those believers were so happy they were selling their houses and bringing the proceeds to the apostles, and they were meeting the needs of the people; and there was a great expression of sacrifices on the part of the believers. God blesses that in a church.

Don't you like to be in a place where you don't always have to be begging folks, "Now, you're behind on your giving, and if you don't give, we're going to have to turn the lights out next Wednesday night, and we can't have a service, and come on, you all have to give"?

Dr. Lindsay, Sr., in the early 1940s established a policy in our church that we pay as we go. God has blessed our church with marvelous facilities which have cost multi-millions of dollars. People come and visit and preachers write, and they ask, "Well, how are you financing that?"

And I reply, "What do you mean?"

"Well, how are you raising money?"

"Well, we're not raising any money. It's already paid for."

"It is? What kind of campaign did you have to get that kind of money?"

I explain, "We didn't have a campaign. Our people believe and obey Bible. When God's people believe it and obey it, needs are met."

There was also not only a unity in experience and a unity of expression, there was a *unity of evangelism*. Verse 33: "And with great power gave the apostles witness of the resurrection of the Lord Jesus: and great grace was upon them all." The verse starts with great power, and it closes out with great grace. And sandwiched right in between those two is the matter of witnessing faithfully for the Lord Jesus.

If you begin to be a witness for Jesus, your witness will be attended by great power and great grace in unusual measure. I started winning people to the Lord when I was about 16 years old. I have had some interesting and wonderful experiences. I am not an expert soul-winner. I am still learning how to be a better witness for the Lord.

I remember during the days of the "hippie" movement. People become all upset about men's long hair. Somebody said, "Are you worried about hair?" I said, "No, I'm not worried about people's hair as much as I'm worried about their hearts. If people get their hearts right, they'll get their hair right." And I'm at the stage where I admire men who can grow hair anywhere they can grow it. I was witnessing to a young guy who was deeply involved in the hippie movement, and he had a live-in girlfriend. Does that sound familiar?

One night I witnessed to him and his lover. And it seemed there was nothing that could break through. I had prayer and left. In the wee hours of the night he called and asked me to come back. About 2 o'clock in the morning I arrived at their "pad." The power of God was so real that the girl was so much under the convicting power of God that she was shaking literally so hard the sofa was bouncing up and down off the floor. God came down. They were saved! And that young man is a psychologist today; he is counseling people and helping them meet problems in their lives.

Oh, the power of God! Ask God to use you as a soul-winner, and the power of heaven will come to bear upon your life. God will pour His grace into your life. Every day becomes an adventure. Whatever job you have becomes an opportunity for you to win people to the Lord. You work in an office somewhere, and you're the only Christian there. Wonderful! God has given you the opportunity to be a missionary for Jesus. Are you in a factory, and the language is vile and the atmosphere, ungodly? Great! Because God's favor will come upon you if you will be a witness for Jesus there.

The church—*the total church*. Let's zoom in now and move closer.

The Matter of the Personal Church

A church is made up of people. The church is not a building. The church is not a program. A church is people! You knew that when you were little. It used to be like this: "Here's the church, and there's the steeple, open the door, and there's the people." Remember that? That is biblical! A church is individuals and a church exists for people. It changes people; wins people; matures people. We are in the people business, and that's why every decision we make here pivots around the question, "How will it win people? How will it help people to grow in the Lord?"

The purpose of a church is not primarily for entertainment. If you are in an alive church, it can be entertaining. But all kinds of exciting and unusual things can happen. It's entertaining, but that's not the purpose of the church. The purpose of the church is not to elevate your intellect, though it's educating to attend church. A person who attends a Bible-believing, Bible teaching church can get an education. Winston Churchill wrote, in essence, that no man has a right to consider himself truly educated until he has a working knowledge of the Word of God. The Word of God becomes the touchstone of all truth. Everything should be measured by the standard of the Word of God.

Young people, when you go off to school, keep your Bible in one hand, your textbooks in the other, and measure all you read, all you see, all you hear alongside the authority of the Word of God. If what you hear is in keeping and in harmony with the Bible, it's truth. If it is contradictory to the Bible, it is error and not truth. Jesus said, "Thy word is truth."

It is not the purpose of a church to improve you culturally, though it should enhance your culture to become a Christian. I think being a Christian means you ought to take a bath and use deodorant, huh? It's good to learn some social graces and to become gentlemanly and ladylike in one's life.

The purpose of a church is to help people become Christ-like, growing in the image of Jesus. Now, that's what predestination is all about. Has God predestined some to go to heaven and others to go to hell? Predestination is a family truth for believers. In Romans 8:29, Paul wrote that God "hath He predestinated, that you might be conformed to the image of his son." That means God predetermines that every person who is saved shall ultimately become like the Lord Jesus Christ!

We are going to be just like Jesus one of these days! We shall see Him, and we shall be like Him for we shall see Him as He is (see 1 John 2:2b). But between now and then, the church is to help me become more like Jesus.

In this early church the Spirit of God gives us a quick snapshot of a believer who was Exhibit A of the kind of Christian the early church was producing, and his name was "Barnabas."

Look at this personal Christian for a moment. Verse 36: "And Joses, who by the apostles was surnamed Barnabas, (which is, being interpreted, The son of consolation) . . ." Look at his character for a moment. Barnabas was surnamed by the church. The church gave him a nickname. Different translations put it differently. Some claim Barnabas means "the son of consolation," as the King James does. Others translate it as Barnabas, "the son of encouragement." I like *The Living Bible*. It calls him "Barney the Preacher." Not bad either. But the one that really appeals to me is Barnabas, "the son of refreshment." He was a refreshing Christian. Other believers in the fellowship looked at Barnabas and exclaimed, "Man, he's a refreshing Christian!"

What's your name around the church? There are all kinds of nicknames for folks around the church. "Yep. There goes Herman the Hypocrite!" He comes to church, sings the loudest of anybody, prays the longest, and he makes sure everybody sees him. He cusses unbelievably on the job. He's a mockery of the name of the Lord Jesus Christ.

And then, "Oh yeah, she came in too, didn't she? There she is—Worldly Wilma." It doesn't matter what the Bible or what the standards of Christ-like conduct are. Whatever the world dictates, that's what Wilma does. If the style is to put a gold ring in your nose, Wilma will be the first one to get one. Worldly Wilma. She has sold out to the world. Everybody knows her.

And then "Who's that coming in? Oh, yeah, uh huh, yeah, yeah, I know him. Gary Gripe." It doesn't matter if the choir sings a slow number, it's, "Man, I wish they'd sing a fast one." If they sing a fast one, it's, "Boy, I'll tell you, I'm tired of those fast ones. I wish they'd sing a slow one." If it's cool in here, he wishes it were warmer. If it's warm in here, he would gripe, gripe, gripe . . . Nobody likes to sit around Gary.

And then here's Indifferent Ida. She just doesn't care. You could have a thousand people saved Sunday morning. Ida doesn't care. "Who cares? I'm just old Indifferent Ida, I'm just along for the ride!"

Then there's Smutty Sam. Watch him. He'll tell you one of those double-entendre jokes. And if you object to it, he'll say, "Well, you've got a dirty mind." If you laugh at it, you compromise your Christian testimony. He has failed to obey the scriptural injunction not to let corrupt communication proceed out of your mouth. A believer ought never leave any question by his language or conversation that he does not belong totally to the Lord Jesus. Shame on you, Smutty Sam.

There is Prideful Polly. She's Miss Big Shot around the church. "Look at me! My husband's a deacon! I am Prideful Polly!"

Then there's Rebellious Ralph. He's a teenager. "Mama's making me come to church, and when I get big I ain't going to church no more." Yeah, Ralph, mama made you take a bath too, didn't she? I guess when you grow up you'll quit bathing too and smell up the whole world.

Motor Mouth Mildred normally sits in the balcony, and don't sit around her, closer than ten rows, or you won't hear a thing in the service. How can you cure Motor Mouth Mildred? The next time you sit around her and she starts talking, look around and give her a stern look and ask, "Would you be quiet, please, so I can hear what's going on?" And if you do it in a serious tone of voice, you'll be surprised how subdued Mildred will become. When I go into a church service and sit down and someone starts talking, I say, "I can't hear what they're saying. Would you please be quiet?"

What's your church nickname? Thank God there are some others. Thank God for Prayerful Pam. She faithfully prays for her church every day.

And then there's Faithful Frank. He may not be the most gifted or the most well to do, but when the doors are open, Frank's there. He's faithful to the Lord, to his church, to the Word of God.

Then there's Consecrated Carol. She has totally committed her life to the Lord. And then there's Working Walter. Need a job done? Just give it to Walter. He'll work day and night for the love of Jesus Christ.

I wish my name could be Barnabas. I wish I could be known as "the son of refreshment." Wouldn't it be wonderful to be the kind of Christian that folks talk about like this? "You know what? Being around that Christian is like taking a good, cool drink of water on a hot summer day."

Paul wrote about many of those. Romans 15:32: "That I may come unto you with joy by the will of God, and may with you be refreshed." First Corinthians 16:18, "For they have refreshed my spirit and yours." Second Timothy 1:16, "The Lord give mercy unto the house of Onesiphorus; for he oft refreshed me, and was not ashamed of my chain." Philemon 7, "For we have great joy and consolation in thy love, because the bowels of the saints are refreshed by thee, brother." Let's pray that God will make us a Christian like Barnabas.

When you follow the life of Barnabas you will note he was consistently an encourager, a consoler, a refresher. For instance, he took everything he had and gave it to the church. Let's follow

Barnabas around for a while. In Acts 9 we read about the conversion of Saul. Saul was saved, but some doubters were around. Look at Acts 9:26: "And when Saul was come to Jerusalem, he assayed [that is, he tried] to join himself to the disciples: but they were all afraid of him and believed not that he was a disciple." But Barnabas accompanied Saul to meet the apostles "and declared unto them how he had seen the Lord in the way and that he had spoken to him and how he had preached boldly at Damascus in the name of Jesus" (v. 27). Barnabas had a new Christian under his shoulder, encouraging him. Refreshing!

"Then tidings of these things came unto the ears of the church which was in Jerusalem: and they sent forth Barnabas, that he should go as far as Antioch. Who, when he came, and had seen the grace of God, was glad, and exhorted them all, that with purpose of heart they would cleave unto the Lord" (Acts 11:22). He had enough spiritual insight to tell when the grace of God was at work in a fellowship. How refreshing!

In Chapter 15:36 and following we are told that Barnabas, who had now become the missionary companion of Paul, came to a difference of opinion about a young man named John Mark. John Mark was one of those Christians who started well but faltered midway in his service for the Lord. When it came time to go on another journey, verse 37 states: "And Barnabas determined to take with him John, whose surname was Mark."

In verse 38 Paul would have nothing to do with that at all. Paul felt John Mark was a dismal failure. He argued with Barnabas: "You're not going to give him another chance. He blew it; he went running home to mama right in the heat of the battle." Verse 39, "And the contention was so sharp between them that they departed asunder one from another: and so Barnabas took

Mark, and sailed unto Cyprus." Barnabas was the kind of Christian who was willing to give people a second chance. How refreshing!

Don't you want to be a refreshing person? Wouldn't you rather be one of those people that others rush up to instead of run away from? Wouldn't you want to be so much like Jesus, and have such an attractiveness and winsomeness about your Christian life, that when people come around you, they'd walk away saying, "Just like a good drink of cold well water!" Jesus can make you that kind of Christian!

4
Growing a Great Church

The church is not a passive, milquetoast organization to be tossed about by the whims of a pagan world. But the church is a militant, aggressive army, marching against the enemy . . . The battle is won. The victory is ours. . . . That is the church. Militant! Aggressive! Victorious!

—James T. Draper, Jr.

Acts 9:31

Then had the churches rest throughout all Judea and Galilee and Samaria, and were edified; and walking in the fear of the Lord, and in the comfort of the Holy Ghost, were multiplied.

Dr. Luke from time to time stops and gives us a review of what has gone on in the previous chapters. He is climbing a mountain, comes to a plateau, takes a breather, and looks back. He files progress statements of the development of the early church—a bird's-eye view, a little cameo concerning church growth.

J. B. Phillips referred to the Book of Acts as an "infant's progress." It is the picture of the birth, the growth, and the development of the baby church. As you study Acts you will discover the basic principles and procedures revealed by the Holy Spirit to build a dynamic body of Christ.

Early on in my ministry the Lord led me to a careful study of Acts, and in that study, the Lord showed me the basic tenets of building a New Testament church that will apply in every age, in every circumstance, in every situation. If you adopt these principles and apply them correctly, I believe the Lord will help you to grow a church anywhere.

In this verse of Scripture we have the picture of the early church in perfect balance. The churches were edified. There was spiritual growth in the churches. The churches were also multiplied. Something was going on inside and outside of the fellowship.

Sadly, there is a tendency for churches to get out of balance. If we are not careful, we will always be on one side of the seesaw. There is a tendency for us to beat on the drum with only one stick, and so we tend to lose our balance. Sometimes churches go to extremes, and all they emphasize is evangelism—winning the lost to Christ. Of course, we know that is the priority assignment. The Lord Jesus specifically commanded us to make disciples. But, you see, the church is not just all "go." The church is also "grow." And, it is a responsibility for a church to help converts grow and mature in their Christian life. So, when a church goes to the extreme of emphasizing only evangelism to the exclusion of a church growth development plan for its members, then that church produces a generation of spiritual pygmies. It's sort of like folks who go fishing; they have good bait and a good hook, but they don't have a rod and reel to bring them in and tie them into the fellowship of a New Testament congregation. So that's one extreme of churches.

The other extreme is when people tend to go into the direction of discipleship, and the whole emphasis of the church becomes that. And they talk mostly about feeding the sheep. Of course, we know that is exactly what the Lord teaches us to do. The Lord rebuked His disciple, Simon Peter, with: "If you love me, feed my sheep." But, being a pastor for about thirty years or more, I have learned some characteristics of sheep. There is a tendency for sheep to run off into somebody else's pasture, and so you have to watch the sheep all along. And, then there is also a tendency for some sheep to stray and so you don't have the opportunity to feed those sheep. Of course, some sheep die along the way. If you are not reaching more sheep, you are going to find out that you will be feeding fewer and fewer sheep. Yes, we are to help those who are saved to mature in the Lord. But you cannot go to extremes and neglect the evangelistic imperative which the Lord has given to His church.

So, that brings me to emphasize that in 9:31 there was an ingenious balance in a New Testament congregation. There are two verbs in this verse which are the load-bearing verbs of the statement. The churches were *edified* and then were *multiplied*. So, first of all, let's discuss inward edification, the building up of the Body of Christ. The word edified is the same word that means to build up. We use that word sometimes when we refer to a church building as the edifice. That is the building, and it is a beautiful figure of speech concerning what is intended to go on inside a church. Now the apostle Paul used that same figure of speech. There is a definite connection between Acts and Ephesians. Paul utilized many meaningful figures of speech to describe the church. Sometimes he compared the church to a body. That reminds us of the function of a church. On other occasions he referred to the church as a bride. And that reminds us of our fidelity to the church.

We are to love the church and we are to be faithful to the Head of the church. But the Lord, through Paul, also presents the church as a building. Look at Ephesians 2:19:

> Now therefore ye are no more strangers and foreigners, but fellow-citizens with the saints and of the household of God; And are built upon the foundation of the apostles and prophets, Jesus Christ himself being the chief corner stone.

That statement points us to the foundation of the building, the church. Do not misread what is here. He is not saying that the apostles and the prophets are the foundation, but that they laid the foundation. They did the foundational work of the church. The apostles were the great architects of the church. The apostle Paul in fact says that in 1 Corinthians 3. Paul called himself a "wise master builder." It is the Greek word from which we derive our English word "architect." Paul said, "I am a wise architect." And then he said, "I have laid the foundation; other men are building their own. Take heed now you build their own. And then he wrote in verse 11—"For other foundation can no man lay than that which is laid, which is Jesus Christ." Ladies and gentlemen, the foundation of the church is none other than the Lord Jesus Christ Himself. A building is only as strong as the foundation upon which it is laid.

When I attended school in New Orleans several years ago, I remember going down on Canal Street. I saw a scene I had never seen in all my life. They were about to build a building, and on the building site they had a pile of telephone poles. With a huge machine they were driving them into the ground. And after they drove one into the ground, they put another pole on top of that one and they drove it into the ground. I discovered that because of the kind of soil in that particular area, it was necessary for them to go down deep until finally they hit solid rock because they knew they could not build a magnificent building until first of all there was an adequate foundation. The problem in many places is that pastors are trying to build a skyscraper church on a chicken coop foundation! If you try to build a church on anything except the Lord Jesus Christ, that church ultimately is destined to fail. A church stands on the Lord, or it does not stand at all.

After Simon Peter's confession, "Thou art the Christ, the Son of the living God," Jesus came back with this: "and I say also unto thee, that thou art Peter [a little pebble], and upon this rock [a big stone] I will build my church and the gates of hell shall not prevail against it" (Matt. 16:18). The church is founded upon nothing other than the person and the provision of Jesus Christ in His shed blood. That is how you build a church.

You don't build a church on music. I thank God for music. I love music. I love all of our musicians. I love singing and playing. There are some folks who try to do that, you know. "Come on over to our church tonight, the Ball Bearing Four is going to sing." They bawl and you bear it. Also don't build a church on the personality of the preacher, either. People have the idea today if our preachers can be as slick as Madison Avenue and they can be personalities, you can build a church. You can't build a church on the personality of a pastor. And you can't build a church on gimmicks and programs, either.

I remember hearing the late Vance Havner tell about a church that was having "Super Sunday." And he said they had Ed the Wonder Horse that day for Super Sunday. They led Ed the Wonder Horse up there and said, "All right, Ed, how much is one plus one, and he stomped two times. The little kids' eyes all bugged out. And then Ed was asked how much is two plus two, and he stomped four times, and now the adults' eyes popped out of their sockets. Then Ed was queried, "How many hypocrites are in this church?" and the horse broke into a trot. You can build a crowd and a certain kind of excitement with gimmicks, but, friend, the only way you can build a genuine church is to establish it on the Lord Jesus Christ. And the church that is founded and grounded on the Lord Jesus Christ is a church that is destined to stand until the Lord comes again. But then I want you to notice in verse 21 how a church is to be framed. "In whom all the building fitly framed together groweth unto an holy temple in the Lord." He speaks about how that structure of the church is to go up. I want to suggest several tools given to us in the New Testament that can be used to frame the building of the church, to build up that building of the Lord in the local fellowship.

The Bible says in 1 Corinthians 14:26—"Let all things be done unto edifying." In other words, all we do at a church ought to be designed to build up, encourage, and to strengthen God's people. Now I will reach into the Lord's tool chest and share with you some tools that God uses to build up His church. The first tool I want to pick up is in Jude 20, where the Bible says, "Building up yourselves on your most holy faith." You build a church by teaching the people to have . . .

Great Faith in God

There is a beautiful picture over in Romans 1:8, where the Bible says, "Your faith is spoken of throughout the world." There was a church famous for its faith. Now churches become famous for all kinds of qualities, don't they? Some churches are famous for their fussing. They are fighting and fussing all the time. Other churches become famous for their facilities. "Come over and see our marvelous chandelier, our activities building." Other churches get famous for their fanaticism. "Come on over and roll on the floor and foam at the mouth with us."

But here was a church famous for faith. Their good reputation spread. We have the glorious opportunity of serving and working with a multitude of people in our church, people who have great faith in God. Our people believe that if God wants it done, there is nothing this church can't do. You must build a church on great faith. The average church does what they think they are able to do. A church famous for faith does what it trusts God to be able to do.

I remember when this church was being built. I was pastor in Mobile, Alabama, and you realize news spreads around the country rapidly and people commented, "Those people over in Jacksonville made a terrible mistake. Oh, they are building a huge building, seats 3,500 or more people, and they are going to move out of a little building that seats 1,200. Tssk, Tssk. They'll never fill the building like that." The first Sunday the dear people of this church walked into the new building, there weren't enough pews to seat all of the people. It wasn't long until they started having two services in this building. We are going to build more facilities right behind here to seat 10,000.

You say, "You're crazy." No, we're not crazy; many of our people have great faith in God. We have enough faith to believe if God wants it built, it will be built because He wants us to fill it up with lost people who can hear the Gospel and be saved. You build a church on tremendous faith in God. You build a church with . . .

Great Love for God

First Corinthians 8:1 says, "Knowledge puffeth up." I doubt if there has ever been a truer statement than that. Knowledge puffeth up. I was pastor for over eight years about a mile from a Baptist college, and I've been in an academic atmosphere most of my life. But, unless handled prayerfully, knowledge can inflate one's ego—puff them up like a lovesick bullfrog. I have heard, "Some folks are educated beyond their intelligence." "Knowledge puffeth up." But the rest of the statement says, "But love builds up." Love edifies. God uses love in a fellowship to build up the believers.

The church ought to be the most loving place in all of the world. People in this world are starving for love. A few years ago I heard a country song that went, "Looking for love in all the wrong places." That's an apropos statement, isn't it? That's what people are doing—they are looking for love, but they are looking for it in all the wrong places. Those love seekers are filling up bars and lounges and finding laughter and lights and liquor and lust, and some other l's I could mention, but they are not finding any real love. The only place this old sin-sick world, this love-starved world, is going to find love is in a church where the love of the Lord Jesus Christ is. People have a right to find love in the house of the Lord. Jesus said, "by this shall all men know that you are my disciples if you have love one for another." This world is starving for love.

I heard about a little boy in the children's home who was causing problems. He was a constant pest. The officials in the home were looking for an excuse to move him on to another home and get him out of their hair. And I remember one day they saw the little boy steal across the grounds, climb up a tree, and deposit something in one of the branches, and then steal away, and they thought, "Aha, now we've got him. Now, there's our excuse to get rid of this troublemaker boy." And, as soon as the boy had stolen away, they rushed to the tree, climbed up, and in the branches of the tree they opened up a note the boy had written. On the note it said, "If anybody finds this, I love you."

I have a feeling that some of the irresponsible behavior we are witnessing from unsaved people out there is nothing in the world but those people crying out, "If anybody finds me, I love you." And it would be a shame for a poor lost sinner to attend a church and not find the love of Jesus.

One of my preacher boys was a bus pastor at a church in Nashville, Tennessee, several years ago and had talked to people who had worked in bus ministries. You know how hectic that can be. The church was having a big Sunday. They had droves of kids coming in on buses, and he was the leader of the ministry. All through the morning a little boy was bugging him to death. Every time he'd turn around he ran into the little boy. Whenever he tried to move, the boy was pulling on his coat and saying, "Mr. Ziger, Mr. Ziger."

Finally, almost at the end of the morning the persistent boy grabbed hold of Ziger's knee, and he said, "Mr. Ziger, Mr. Ziger." Almost out of patience he looked down at the boy and said, "Son, what do you want?" And the fellow replied, "Mr. Ziger, I just want you to love me!" Listen, friend, you build a church with love. We try to teach our people here to love the Lord Jesus, because if we can persuade our people to fall in love with the Lord Jesus, we believe they will fall in love with one another. We feel as if we have found the solution to the racial problem in this country. Because, you see, in our fellowship it doesn't matter what your social standing may be. Or your racial background or where you come from. It really doesn't matter where you are on the scale academically. You see, the love of Jesus is in this place.

And when you get white folks, black folks, yellow folks, and brown folks, in love with the Lord Jesus Christ, then Jesus can teach them to love one another. Love builds a church. Not only does *faith* build a church, not only does *love* build a church, but building a church requires . . .

Great Spiritual Gifts

First Corinthians 14:12—"Even so ye, forasmuch as ye are zealous of spiritual gifts, seek that ye may excel to the edifying of the church." You are aware the Bible teaches that every believer has one or more spiritual gifts. And the Bible teaches that those spiritual gifts are to be used by individual believers to edify the body of Christ, to build up believers. Spiritual gifts are not toys to play with, but tools to build with. Thank God for the army of people in our fellowship and yours who are using the spiritual gifts God has given them to build up the body of Jesus Christ.

Of course, some people's gifts are more prominent and outward than others. God gives some gifts of music, and they use it to build up the body. Others have the gift of ushering, and they use it. Those are sometimes called helps. How important those gifts are. Others have the gifts of teaching and preaching, and those gifts are vitally important. But there are other people who exercise gifts that are more in the background. God bless those people who are willing to spend a little time in the preschool department, caring for some young couple's baby so that young couple can come into the services, hear the Gospel, and get saved. If people start exercising their gifts in the church, the church of the Lord will be built up.

When I was in Rome, Georgia, we conducted a revival with Dr. Homer Lindsay, Jr. At the particular time we were running about 600 in Sunday School and we were getting ready to launch toward 1,000. I asked Homer to help with a special Sunday School teachers and officers meeting. I said, "Now after the service on Monday night I'm going to have all my Sunday School teachers and officers in a meeting, and I want you to tell them how we can get our church to grow from 600 to over 1,000." Man, I had visions. Homer was going to lay it on the line for them. We had a big map and chart—the works.

I was going to have a full two-hour Sunday School clinic right there. I said, "Now I'll greet the people at the door as they enter. You go ahead and get the meeting started, and I'll be back there." It took me about five minutes to greet the people, and I returned where my members were sitting in rapt attention ready for the full Sunday School clinic. They were simply sitting there. Not a word being said. Homer and my folks were just looking at one another.

I suggested, "Well, it's time to start the meeting," and Homer replied, "We've already had it."

"Already had it?" He answered, "Yep, it's already over."

I said, "I want you to tell these folks how we can get the Sunday School to go from 600 to 1,000. I've already done it."

And I said, "Well, what did you say?"

"I just told them they had to be like the ants. Do you remember that?"

"You've got to be kidding!"

He repeated himself, "I just told them they've got to be like the ants. You see, every ant has got an assignment and every ant carries out its assignment. That's the way you have to be in a church. Takes a lot of people to do God's business in a church. Takes Sunday School teachers. Takes group leaders, outreach leaders, and in all of that—you see spiritual gifts have been given by the Holy Spirit to individual believers, but in order to use them as tools to build the church of the Lord Jesus Christ."

Oh, yes, spiritual gifts. Not only do spiritual gifts build a church but . . .

Great Preaching

First Corinthians 14:4 says, "He that prophesieth edifieth the church." And in our situation today he is talking about preaching. A few years ago the prophets of doom announced the end of preaching. They pronounced the demise of preaching. The preaching of the gospel was going to be ineffective. They claimed we have to have drama and we have to have dialogue and we must have symposiums and we must have talkbacks. I'll agree there's an abundance of dead preaching.

Did you hear about the pastor who was preaching from his notes up there? Along came a gust of wind and blew his notes out the window. A cow came along and ate his notes, and the cow dried up! Yes, I agree, there's too much dead preaching.

I heard about two laymen uptown on a Monday morning after the Sunday services. One of them said to the other, "Well, how was the preaching over at your place Sunday?" The other layman came back with, "Oh, my, it was the same old *ding-dong, ding-dong.*"

And the other one said, "Well, you ought to be thankful. At our church it was the same old *ding-ding, ding-ding.*" The day of preaching is not dead. When a man of God will get filled with the Spirit of God, bury his heart and mind in the Word of God, stand up in the house of God, and preach faithfully to the people of God, the glory of God will come down. I still believe in the power of the preaching of the Word of God. I expect miracles to happen when the gospel of the Lord Jesus is proclaimed. Let me encourage you today—let's preach the Word correctly, consistently, courageously, and compassionately. Let's preach the Word with all of the fervency of our hearts and when the Word is preached, the people will be built up and they will walk out fed by the Bread of Life. When I look over the congregation many times I think about the fact that there may be 3,000 or more people here, and if I'm going to preach thirty minutes, multiply all of that, and that's about 1,500 hours of time. God have mercy on me if I take 1,500 hours of people's time and do not give them the Word of God. There is nothing like preaching. The grandest occasion in a week's time is when you walk into the pulpit and open up the Word and preach that Word to the congregation. I speak to my preacher friends. You may not be the greatest preacher in the world, but you are *God's preacher* wherever you are. I remember hearing about an old preacher from the country, Brother John. Somebody asked him, "John, who's the greatest preacher you ever heard?" John thought for a minute, "You know, well . . . I'll tell you what, when he's wired up to heaven, I just about soon hear old John as anybody I know." That's how I feel, Brother. When you really have the anointing of God on you, it makes all the difference. When you are wired up to heaven, when you are preaching, and the power of God comes down, it's wonderful, isn't it?

Verse 22 declares, "You are also built together for inhabitation of God through the Spirit." That's how the building is filled. You see, you have to put the building on a foundation. You have to frame the building correctly, and when you have done it all correctly, then the Bible indicates the building becomes a habitation for God through the Spirit. In the Old Testament when they built the building according to a pattern, when they put it together as God had instructed them, when all of the pieces of the building were properly in place, then the glory of God came down upon that place. When you build a church on Jesus, and when you build a church on the things that edify, the glory of God comes down in that church. Then were the churches edified. That's the inward ministry of a church.

Return to Acts 9:31. "Then had the churches rest and were edified." And then it says, "And walking in the fear of the Lord, and in the comfort of the Holy Ghost, were multiplied." *Inward edification, outward multiplication.* You see, when God has done something in a church, then He can do something through a church. When something has happened on the inside of the walls, then something can happen on the outside of the walls. Churches were multiplied. That is the second time that particular word is used in the Book of Acts. It is also used back in Acts 6:7, the account of the ordination of the deacons: "And the word of God increased; and the number of the disciples multiplied." Same word. You may say, "Preacher, how does that happen? How is a church multiplied? How are people won to the Lord Jesus?"

Acts 5:42 is a summary statement: "And daily in the temple, and in every house, they ceased not to teach and preach Jesus Christ." They won people to the Lord publicly—in the temple. All of our services are soul-winning services. In every service we give an invitation for people to accept Jesus as their Lord and Savior. And you see, it is important that people bring lost friends to the services. When I finished preaching at an 8 AM service and gave the invitation, a whole row of girls, eight of junior-high age, came down the aisle. When they were presented to the congregation that morning, two of our girls in the church here talked about the slumber party they had. I don't know why they call them slumber parties—they never sleep in them. They had invited their friends and at that slumber party they had led six of their friends to Jesus, and the next morning they brought them down front to make their public professions of faith in the Lord. If little girls can do that, grown men can certainly do that.

Get people to the services under the preaching of the Gospel. You will win people publicly. You can be multiplied publicly. But then note: "And in every house." In every house. That is interesting, because you find the same approach in Acts 20:20 where Paul says, "I have taught you publickly, and from house to house."

You say, "Well, preacher, give me that in the *New International Version.*" "House to house."

"Preacher, I'd like to have that in *The Living Bible.*"

"House to house."

"Preacher, give me the original Greek on that." "House to house." "You mean knocking on doors?" Yes. "Like an encyclopedia salesman?" Yes. House to house. "Like a milkman?" Yes. House to house. You say, well, it won't work. It will work. You can't improve on the methods of Jesus. You see, it's not that the method won't work; it's that the method has been found difficult, and we have quit doing it. There is nothing like going out with a prospect card in your hand, fumbling around, trying to find an address in the night. Cold night. Going up there and knocking on a door or ringing a doorbell, walking into a house, and there's an old smelly carpet and a flea-bitten sofa over here, beer cans scattered all over the place, and then sitting down in that home and taking the New Testament, and step-by-step showing that old boy he's a sinner, that he's going to hell, that Jesus loved him enough to go to a cross that he might be saved, and that if he will repent of his sins and receive Jesus Christ as his personal Savior, he can be saved. And see that old boy get down on his knees and accept Jesus. There is nothing in this world as exciting as that.

When I was a fifteen-year-old boy, our pastor had gone to the Holy Land. If you want to ruin a pastor, send him to the Holy Land. So our assistant pastor was in charge. We were having a revival meeting in a little mission we operated. And he said, "I'm going to take you out visiting with me. I said, "I'll go, but I ain't gonna say nothing." So, we went into a home of two teenage boys. The assistant pastor looked at me and clammed up. Speechless. So I finally figured out if I didn't say something we'd never get out of there. I remember our pastor giving us a few verses about the plan of salvation. I stumbled through those verses. I was terrible. So, finally in utter defeat and frustration I looked at those two boys and I asked, "You wouldn't want to get saved, would you?" And to my utter surprise both of them said, "yes." We saw both of those teenaged boys saved.

The next Sunday night I was sitting in the congregation and saw those guys come through the baptistry. I can't explain it. It's in the realm of the mystical as far as I'm concerned. When I saw that, something started burning down in my soul. God built a fire in me. He gave me a desire to see people come to know Jesus Christ. To this very day, over thirty-five years later, the fire has never stopped burning. I want to see people saved with all the fervor of my heart. And that's how you build a church. The churches were edified. *Inward edification*. And the churches were multiplied. *Outward multiplication*.

5
The Making of an Apostle

He (Paul) is Christ's master soul-winner. His influence in the world today is next to Christ's. He is God's most powerful human advocate and exponent. His is Christ's noblest witness. He ranks first in the world's long list of evangelists. He said he was the chief of sinners. The world says he is chief of saints.

—L. R. Scarborough

Acts 9:21-30

But all that heard him were amazed, and said; Is not this he that destroyed them which called on this name in Jerusalem, and came hither for that intent, that he might bring them bound unto the chief priests? But Saul increased the more in strength and confounded the Jews which dwelt at Damascus, proving that this is the very Christ. And after that many days were fulfilled, the Jews took counsel to kill him: But their laying in wait was known of Saul. And they watched the gates day and night to kill him. Then the disciples took him by night, and let him down by the wall in a basket. And when Saul was come to Jerusalem, he assayed to join himself to the disciples: but they were all afraid of him, and believed not that he was a disciple. But Barnabas took him, and brought him to the apostles, and declared unto them how he had seen the Lord in the way, and that he had spoken to him, and how he had preached boldly at Damascus in the name of Jesus. And he was with them coming in and going out at Jerusalem. And he spake boldly in the name of the Lord Jesus, and disputed against the Grecians: but they went about to slay him. Which when the brethren knew, they brought him down to Caesarea and sent him forth to Tarsus.

In verse 16 of this chapter the Lord declared that Saul was "a chosen vessel unto the Lord to bear his name before Gentiles and kings, and the children of Israel." Even the greatest men and women are merely vessels that God has condescended to use.

In 2 Corinththians 4:7—"We have this treasure in earthen vessels, that the excellency of the power may be of God, and not of us." When God uses an individual it means God has reached down and used an humble person and filled him with His power. In 2 Timothy 2, the Bible compares the believer to a vessel in a mansion where there are vessels of gold, wood, and clay. Each vessel is to be fit for the Master's use.

The implication of that imagery is that God chooses to mold and shape those vessels into what He intends them to be. God had reached down in the mire and saved this man Saul. Having saved him, He began to shape him into the vessel He had destined him to become. In the early years after his conversion, there were four geographical locations that played prominent roles in his life. In each one of those places, God used a different method to mold him into God's vessel. Understand that whatever God does in our lives, He will employ a method to make us useful for Him. First of all, God sent Saul to Arabia. Look at verse 23: "Then after that many days were fulfilled."

Sometimes the Bible compresses a long time into a brief span of Scripture, as is the case right here: "After many days." When you compare Acts 9 to Galatians 1, you will discover that "many days" actually stretched into several years. In Galatians 1:1, Paul gives us little insight into what God did for him in those early days of his conversion. In Galatians 1:15, Paul wrote: "But when it pleased God who separated me from my mother's womb and called me by his grace, to reveal His Son in me, that I might preach him among the heathen."

Then he testified, "Immediately I conferred not with flesh and blood: Neither went I up to Jerusalem" [that is, not at that time] "to them which were apostles before me: but I went into Arabia."

Solitude in Arabia

God was going to use the method of solitude in Saul's life. Arabia is mostly desert, in the Sinai peninsula, a place of solitude and barrenness where Saul would be alone for three years.

Many characters in the Bible had also gone into that same area to be taught of God. *Moses* walked on those desert sands and there beheld the burning bush. There Moses received the Law from the hand of the Lord. There God revealed to him the tabernacle that would be the worship center for God's people in the wilderness. In Moses' Sinai experience, God did a work in his life.

Elijah evidently sojourned in the same area. Elijah knew what it was to go through a season of despair. He was so dejected he cried to the Lord, "Take my life, I don't want to live anymore." Yet, in that wilderness experience, in a still small voice God spoke to Elijah, and he was rejuvenated spiritually.

God had used a period of solitude to perform His work in their lives. God often works in this fashion. We remember that the Lord Jesus had a ministry of three years. And, yet, there were periods of solitude—when Jesus worked with His hands in a carpenter's shop, solitude as He meditated upon the Heavenly Father.

There are several reasons why God gives us periods of solitude. Sometimes it allows us to let Jesus speak to one's heart. In Galatians 1:16, Paul said, "Immediately I conferred not with flesh and blood." God was (Saul's) Paul's professor. Formal education is marvelous. I thank God for every opportunity I have had to attend school. I'm grateful for every teacher who has taught me about the Lord. But I have learned some things from Jesus Christ Himself that no teacher could ever have taught me. If you are in Christ, you have all you need. Receive all the education you can, but the most important education is to be Spirit-taught. Go before Him and let Him teach you about His love.

During those days Saul was taught by the Lord Himself. Shut yourself alone with God for a period of time, alone with your Bible. Sincerely study your Bible and listen to the voice of God. You could have a mountaintop experience and literally shape this world for the Lord. Thank God for solitude.

We must keep in mind that Saul had been a student of the Bible all of his life. Yet, Saul, who was an expert in the Scriptures, who probably had committed to memory at least the first five books of the Old Testament, really didn't understand the Bible's teaching. Saul had the idea that man could be saved by keeping the law. So God sent him to Arabia. Out of that experience Paul wrote words like these.

He wrote that what the law could not do, in that it was weak through sinful flesh, God, sending His own Son in the likeness of sinful flesh, did. He came to understand the whole purpose of the Bible. If you don't see Jesus in the Bible, then you have missed the bottom line of the Scriptures. And so in that Arabian experience he saw the passion of Jesus and the power of the gospel. He reflected on Pentecost.

I think that period of solitude was also a time for God to effect a deeper work in Saul's heart. There was a lot of bitterness in his heart, and he had many wrong attitudes. God removed the bad things and inserted the good. When Saul came back, he was more humble. There was a sweetness about him that he had never reflected before. There was love and gentleness about his character.

Listen, maybe God has given you a period of solitude. Someone said, "Saul went into the desert with Moses, the Psalms, and the Prophets in his knapsack and returned with Romans, Galatians, Ephesians, and Philippians in his heart." He had a brand-new Bible. He had a brand-new burden for those who needed to know the Lord. It was a deeper-life conference, a seminary of solitude. Then he had a red-hot heart for souls.

I believe you ought to go deeply into the Bible. I believe you ought to study the Bible as much as you possibly can. I probably have spent a minimum of six hours a day studying the Bible since I was eighteen. Any deeper-life movement, any Bible-study movement that cools off your zeal for winning the lost is basically flawed. I remember when one of my professors and I were good friends, so I sort of kidded him. I mentioned to him one time, "I don't understand you professors. It seems to me that the more you study the Bible, the drier you become. And the more I study the Bible, the hotter I become to win people to the Lord." Well, I was kind of kidding, yet I was also serious at the same time. If you read the Bible, it'll give you a burning heart for the lost.

Sunday School teachers, don't merely prepare a lesson out of a book, or try to impress your class with how many facts you know about the Bible. Rather, study that lesson and pray, and when you enter that class on Sunday morning you ought to be on fire for God, and those people who leave your class ought to find an unsaved person and lead him to Christ. Thank God for Arabia. Now look again at Galatians 1:17: "I went unto Arabia," and then, "I returned again unto Damascus." Now, what method did God use in Damascus?

Suffering in Damascus

There God used suffering. Here, we'll come back to Galatians 1. Also look at Acts 9.

In Acts 9 we have the record of what happened to Saul in Damascus. Look at verse 23—"And after that many days were fulfilled, the Jews took counsel to kill him: But their laying in wait was known to Saul. And they watched the gates day and night to kill him. Then the disciples took him by night, and let him down by the wall in a basket." Can you imagine how humiliating that must have been? There was a great theologian, a scholar, a genius; and he was let down in a basket from a wall for his faith in Jesus. Recall verse 16, "I will shew him how great things he must suffer for my name's sake."

What Saul was experiencing in Damascus was just the beginning of future suffering. God was preparing him for bigger suffering in the future. Are you suffering? I have unusual news for you—probably God is letting you go through trials in order to fortify you for possible trials in the future. Jeremiah opined, "If you run with the horses and they have wearied thee, what will you do in the swelling of the Jordan?" In other words, if you think this is bad, it's going to become worse.

We are living in a world of suffering. God has purposes and reasons for our suffering. God shapes the vessel through suffering. Have you ever noticed how a potter does his work? He molds the vessel and then He puts it in the fire. In the fire He forges into that vessel the strength and the consistency he desires. That is what God does when He allows suffering to enter our lives. He tempers us for the sufferings ahead of us. He makes us more humble and more submissive. He teaches us lessons in suffering that we can learn no other way. Have you found that to be true? I heard about a lady who talked to her pastor. She was going through terrible times. She said to her pastor, "Pastor, pray for me that I won't miss the lessons God has for me in this."

God uses suffering to tailor us, to mold us, to make us the way He wants us to be. I have heard that Pebble Beach, California, is one of the most beautiful places in all the world. Tourists from all over the world come to collect these smooth, rounded stones, but those stones were not always lovely. Those stones were swept up onto the shore and knocked up against the rocky crags along the beach. As that happened over a long period of time, all the rough edges were worn off until finally they were shaped and lovely. God also allows us to be pounded against the shores of suffering that our faith might be purified and strengthened and that we might become strong, sturdy witnesses for Christ. God sent Paul to Arabia and used *solitude*. God sent him back to Damascus and He used *suffering*.

Service in Jerusalem

"Then after three years I went up to Jerusalem to see Peter, and abode with him fifteen days" (Gal. 1:18). Return to Acts 9. I want to tie these two together because here is the total picture.

"And when Saul was come to Jerusalem, he assayed to join himself to the disciples" (Acts 9:26). In other words, one Sunday morning they gave the hymn of invitation, and down the aisle came Saul to move his letter. But the disciples were afraid of him and "believed not that he was a disciple." Keep in mind that this was the man who had persecuted them. In fact, some people in that congregation probably were fatherless because Saul had taken their fathers and had sent them to prison—and women were husbandless because Saul had persecuted and consented to the death of their husbands. And yet he was coming to be a part of the fellowship there. It required an abundance of God's grace for them to trust what God had done in the life of that man Saul.

Thank God for Barnabas. Oh, "son of encouragement," Barnabas. "But Barnabas took him, and brought him to the apostles, and declared unto them how he had seen the Lord in the way, and that he had spoken to him, and how he had preached boldly at Damascus in the name of Jesus" (Acts 9:27). In other words, Saul had a man who took an interest in him. What was God doing in Jerusalem for Saul? Using *service* to shape His vessel in Jerusalem.

God wants to use a local church. Admittedly Saul's situation

was unusual. They were amazed and astounded that this oppo-
nent of the faith had now become a great preacher of the gospel.
It was a strain on their credibility to put confidence in the conversion of this man. Never underestimate the grace of God, the
power of God to transform an individual. Saul was finally accepted in the church, and he was "coming in and he was going
out." He was working in a local church!

I believe the Bible will sustain this, and experience will prove
this to be true. I do not believe you can effectively grow as a
Christian unless you become involved in the ministry of a local
congregation of believers. If that were not true, then why did
God start the church in the first place? The local church is a terrific place to learn about Jesus. I have a feeling that Saul faithfully
served Jesus right there in the church of Jerusalem.

Back to Galatians 1 again. What else happened while he was
there serving the Lord with the people in Jerusalem? Galatians
1:18 reports that he went up to Jerusalem to see Peter. There is a
picture here that doesn't make itself apparent in the King James
Version. Where it states that he went to Jerusalem to see Peter,
the verb "to see" is where we pick up our English word "history,"
and you could read it this way—"He went up to Jerusalem to
history Peter." That means he went to Jerusalem to ask Simon
Peter, "Tell me the story of Jesus."

I would like to have been there. Wouldn't you like to have
seen Saul and Peter there and hear Saul say to Simon, "Simon, I
want you to give me the whole story. Start at the beginning"?
And wouldn't you like to listen to Simon as he started? I guess he
started with the day that his brother, Andrew, came running back
home and said, "Simon, Man, we have found the Christ! The
Messiah!"

And I guess Simon related how the Lord promised He was going to make a rock out of him. Saul must have thought, "Nobody will make a rock out of me. I am as unstable as the shifting sand!"

And then wouldn't you like to have heard Simon Peter as he told about the time he jumped out of the boat and walked on the water to go to Jesus? Maybe Simon Peter confessed, "Saul, I had the most embarrassing experience of my life. I got out there to Jesus and got my eyes on the wind instead of Jesus, and I almost drowned my crazy self. And all the disciples laughed at me because I had been boasting so much."

And do you think maybe he told about how he denied the Lord Jesus? What a time they must have had. They must have laughed and wept and shouted as Simon told the story of Jesus. When a man meets Jesus he never grows tired of hearing the old, old story of Jesus. You may have heard the story of Jesus over and over again, and it was still as fresh and as wonderful the last time you heard it as the first time. God was using *service in Jerusalem* to shape Paul's life. Now there was a fourth location in the life of Saul.

Silence in Tarsus

In verse 21 he says, "Afterwards I came into the regions of Syria and Cilicia." Connect that with Acts 9:30, "Which when the brethren knew, they brought him down to Caesarea, and sent him forth to Tarsus." Four places God used in his early Christian walk: *Arabia* — God used *solitude. Damascus* — God used *suffering. Jerusalem* — God used *service. Tarsus* — God used *silence.*

Tarsus was Saul's hometown. His parents might still have lived there. Can you imagine how it was when Saul returned home? They had sent him to rabbinical school in Jerusalem to sit at the feet of Gamaliel. When he returned, instead of being a brilliant young rabbi, he was an humble preacher of the Nazarene carpenter. Perhaps they even had his funeral. This is still done today. Saul had become a follower of the lowly Jesus.

For a period of time Saul kind of dropped out of the picture. There was a period of silence in Saul's life. We know little about what happened in those years when Saul returned to Tarsus. In fact, all we can do is conjecture. I do think he was a witness for Jesus. There is a passage later on in Acts that talks about churches which were started in Syria and Seleucia. And it is generally believed by scholars that during those silent years, he was a faithful witness to the Lord and won souls to Christ in that area.

You may not be where you want to be for God, and you may not be serving where you would like. You may feel God has forgotten you. But keep on being a witness for Jesus wherever you are. You may think you are in some out-of-the-way place. God is using that period of silence to shape His vessel. Be faithful to Jesus right there, and you'll be surprised what He'll do one of these days. Paul bloomed where God planted him. He was waiting on the Lord. The Bible says, "Commit thy way unto the Lord, trust also in him, and he shall bring it to pass."

Are you in a phase of obscurity? And every now and then do you feel like saying, "Hey, Lord, remember me? It's me down here, Lord. You haven't forgotten where You left me, have you, Lord?"

I remember hearing W. A. Criswell, over forty years pastor of the First Baptist Church of Dallas, when he said that for the first ten years of his ministry he thought God had forgotten him. He was in a little, obscure church. He'd seen how all of his preacher friends were being used in unusual ways. He would pray and cry, "Lord, have you forgotten me? Lord, are you not going to use me?"

And then one day God reached down, picked him up, and put him where He wanted him to be.

God hasn't forgotten you. God knows exactly where you are. Wait on the Lord. Keep serving Jesus. Continue studying your Bible. Pray! Keep on being faithful to the Lord and keep on telling the old, old story of Jesus. One of these days the Master Potter, when He has shaped you the way He wants to do, when it's just right, He'll lift that vessel off the wheel, and He'll put it in the place He wants it.

In Acts 11 these years of silence in Tarsus have gone on. Saul seems to have dropped off the scene, and then in Acts 11:25 here came Barnabas again. God had done a work in Antioch. Barnabas had gone down and had seen that it was a genuine work of grace. God had truly saved those people. They were new in the Lord. Verse 25—"Then departed Barnabas to Tarsus, for to seek Saul: And when he had found him, he brought him unto Antioch." One day Saul opened the door and there stood his old friend, Barnabas. And Barnabas asked, "Saul, where in the world have you been? We've been looking everywhere for you, Saul. Saul, God's done an unusual thing. God has gone up there into Antioch, and He has saved some people, and we have a church full of new Christians who need somebody who has been alone with God in the Word, who can help them grow in the Lord. How about your going up there with me and being a Bible teacher for a while? Soon Saul moved to Antioch, and he was on the firing line for the Lord. God will shape His vessel and may use strange tools. He may use solitude. He may use the time of silence in your life. But when God gets ready, He will pick you up and put you where He wants you. He'll use you for His glory!

6
A Heavenly Ministry on Earth

"Everybody talkin' 'bout heaven ain't goin' there," goes the old black spiritual. Certain people are so preoccupied with heaven that they do no earthly good. Yes, every blood-bought believer is going to heaven, but in the meantime they are to translate heaven into their committed service here on earth. "Oh, what a foretaste of glory divine!"

—Author unknown

Acts 9:32-42

And it came to pass, as Peter passed throughout all quarters, he came down also to the saints which dwelt at Lydda. And there he found a certain man named Aeneas, which had kept his bed eight years, and was sick of the palsy. And Peter said unto him, Aeneas, Jesus Christ maketh thee whole: arise, and make thy bed. And he arose immediately. And all that dwelt at Lydda and Saron saw him, and turned to the Lord. Now there was in Joppa a certain disciple named Tabitha, which by interpretation is called Dorcas: this woman was full of good works and almsdeeds which she did. And it came to pass in those days, that she was sick, and died: whom when they had washed, they laid her in an upper chamber. And forasmuch as Lydda was nigh to Joppa, and the disciples had heard that Peter was there, they sent unto him two men, desiring him that he would not delay to come to them. Then Peter arose and went with them. When he was come, they brought him into the upper chamber: and all the widows stood by him weeping, and shewing the coats and garments which Dorcas made, while she was with them. But Peter put them all forth, and kneeled down, and prayed; and turning him to the body said, Tabitha, arise. And she opened her eyes; and when she saw Peter, she sat up. And he gave her his hand, and lifted her up, and when he had called the saints and widows, presented her alive. And it was known throughout all Joppa; and many believed in the Lord. And it came to pass, that he tarried many days in Joppa with one Simon a tanner.

After Saul's miraculous conversion, it was not long until God changed his name to Paul. The center of attention now turns to Simon Peter, and we look at this marvelous, magnificent preacher of Pentecost.

Remember the Lord's words to Simon Peter: "Thou art Simon, but I will call you Peter, a rock." God was saying, "I'm going to take you, though you are as unstable as the shifting sand, and I'm going to make a rock out of you and use you wonderfully. I am sure there were many days when Simon Peter must have doubted if God would ever be able to do anything with him.

Many people around him looked at his life, at his failures, at his inconsistencies, and wondered if God would ever do anything with him. Now after the resurrection of his Lord, the Day of Pentecost, and the coming of the Holy Spirit, there was an amazing preacher. This saint of God, Simon Peter, was becoming more and more like the Lord. Did you notice in these verses how much like Jesus Simon Peter seemed to be? He was on a preaching tour much like Jesus was. He was healing people. He was preaching the gospel so much like Jesus did. In his mannerisms and in the methods he used, in the words that he spoke, he reminds me of Jesus.

I think the desire of every Christian is that his life might become like that of the Lord Jesus. That's the desire of my heart. I would like to become more like Jesus every day of my life. I fear there are too many qualities in my life that are unlike the Lord Jesus; and I would be pleased if somehow I could grow and mature in my life, so that day by day by day more of the likeness, the beauty, the wonder, and the love of Jesus would be manifested in my life.

God was moving mightily in Paul's life. When we come to the 10th chapter of Acts, we are told in that chapter of a major breakthrough in the gospel to the world. In this chapter the gospel is extended to the Gentiles. In order for this great breakthrough and for the door of salvation to open to the Gentiles, God had to have a human instrument. God's choice, God's divine appointment for that human instrument was Simon Peter.

Simon Peter had some impediments in his life that God was going to have to remove. If he was going to have an absolutely unbiased, unprejudiced ministry to the Gentiles, then God had to work in his life. This is one of the reasons you will notice in verse 43 that Simon Peter dwelt in Joppa at the house of Simon, a tanner. Most Jews would avoid a tanner, a man who worked with dead bodies and their skins. A tanner was considered unclean by orthodox Jews.

But God was moving in Simon Peter's life, preparing him for a special ministry. Day by day, experience by experience, God prepares His people for what He has in store for them. "God leads His dear children along." Right now God is molding and making you for a ministry He wants you to fulfill. Now another reality becomes apparent as we consider these verses. You will discover the varied ministry of the church of the Lord Jesus.

When I was a boy I used to have a kaleidoscope. They were like telescopes that had little colored rocks in them, along with mirrors on the inside. You would turn that kaleidoscope, and it would make all kinds of eyecatching designs. You watched the stones from different perspectives. This passage is almost like a kaleidoscope. Whenever you gaze at this Scripture, you see a new and varied ministry of the church. It illustrates to us a church with a helping hand.

What I'm going to do is glean through these verses and isolate some of the characteristics of a church that is indeed a church of the helping hand. First, I want you to notice that the church has . . .

A Human Ministry

The church is centered in people, interested in human beings, interested in individuals and their needs. Mention is made of "the saints." Names of people are spelled out here. There is Aeneas and Dorcas and the disciples and saints. Not faceless nonentities, but people with personalities, people with feelings, people who have needs. A real church of the Lord Jesus Christ has a people-focused ministry.

We are living in a day of impersonality. Some of our young people are going off to college, and if they go to a very large school, they will soon discover that they are just a number. You are a number punched into a computer somewhere. There is a hollowness about it. But when I read the New Testament and study the life of our Lord, I discover that Jesus was caught up with individuals. He called people by name: Martha, Mary, Zaccheus, Bartimaeus, Peter, James, and on and on. Jesus conducted His ministry for the benefit of individuals.

Especially we know that Jesus died on the cross for individuals. For the whole world one by one, you and me. When Jesus shed His blood, He poured out His life for every person in the history of the world who would come and receive its saving merits. When Jesus died on the cross, He died for Tom and He died for Sue and He died for Mary and He died for Bill and He died for Dan. He died for *you*. Jesus Christ is intensely concerned about individuals. And the church must follow His example. "People who are needing people . . ." The church ought to be interested in young people. Our youth program is phenomenal. We have camps, choir programs, special visitation—just plain fun in Christ. A group of 155 of our youth met yesterday and did survey work. They turned up over 200 families who are prospects for our church. The only answer I can give to people who ask about our church is: it is a miracle of a sovereign God who has chosen to bless a group of folks who love people.

We are interested in little boys and girls and have erected a magnificent building to house our preschool ministry. We want to have an impact on their little lives. And we want their lives to be richer, fuller, sweeter, and more meaningful. We want them growing up to love Jesus because they have come here. We are interested in all ages, all races. We are interested in all people. We are concerned with men and women. We have a terrific senior adult ministry. Jesus' church is one that deeply cares for people.

A few years ago there was a trend to call church buildings the *plant*. People would talk about the church plant, and I never personally liked that terminology—as if a church were churning out plastic toys on the assembly line. No, we are not a plant. We are an organism—a living body. The body of the Lord Jesus. And we are made up of individuals, real flesh-and-blood people. Even as Simon Peter moved among the people of God in his day, we are touching the lives of people. We are tremendously concerned about people. Look at the needs in this passage. Here was a man named Aeneas, on the bed crippled for eight years. Look at the woman named Dorcas—she was dead. View the grieving, crushed loved ones and friends all around. They had needs. And all of us do have needs, don't we?

In your town there is a man who has a rebellious son. Both of them have a need in their lives. And here's a girl whose parents have told her they are fixing to divorce, and she must decide which one of them she is going to live with now. All of them have dire needs. Here's a woman who is an alcoholic, and she started taking social drinks and she took a drink and she took a drink, and finally the drink is taking her. There is nothing in her own innate constituency that can give her the power to break the shackles of alcohol. She has profound needs. A church exists to help people who have needs. Simon Peter was on the lookout for people who had needs. Are you aware of that in this passage? (v. 33). Did you see its statement about Simon Peter when he found a *certain* man named Aeneas? That means Peter was searching for him. He was looking for a person who needed to be helped. Oh, may God help us to be sensitive toward people who have needs. And then, of course, he found some that he wasn't looking for.

You remember the group of people in Joppa. And we are re-
minded that when Dorcas, that beloved saint of God in the fellowship, died, they sent for Peter. They heard that Peter was
nearby in the city of Lydda, and "they sent unto him two men,
desiring him that he would not delay to come to them" (v. 38). In
other words, when they had a need, where did they turn? They
turned to a preacher.

You know where people turn when they have needs. They
call on people who they think can help them. Billy Graham used
to say, "When a person is dying, he doesn't call for his bartender."
They are looking for somebody who knows how to pray, who
has some basic answers to the great problems of life. Janet and I
were watching a television program the other night which dis-
cussed the drug problem in America. As the program began I
said to her, "Now this program is going to tell us exactly what the
needs are. It's going to tell us all about the problem, but it's not
going to give any solutions." And sure enough when the program
was over the network had done a good job telling us how bad a
mess the drug problem is in America. But they didn't have one
specific suggestion about how to solve the problem.

I have a stupendous announcement to make. The church of
the Lord Jesus has the answers to human needs. We have an
answer to the alcohol problem. I thank God for any cure that will
wean a person off liquor. We have a Calvary cure. We believe
that the Lord Jesus Christ has the power to break the shackles of
alcohol. The church has an answer to the drug problem, too.
When I was a nine-year-old boy I was saved, got high on Jesus,
and I've never come down. And I have never seen a drug that
can give you what you receive when you come to the Lord Jesus
Christ. Some runners undergo a "natural high." I know that's
true. And that's why some people get hooked on running—

because the more you run, the longer it takes you to achieve that natural high. And there is such euphoria about that feeling that once you've had it, it's a release. All of a sudden you experience that ethereal feeling. And the more you run, the further along you have to go to experience it, and that's why folks run more and more and more.

I have a natural high that's far better than that. And I'm talking about being filled with the Spirit and in love with the Lord Jesus, having Christ in your life and walking in the power of the Holy Spirit. The church has solutions to the problems they face these days. Oh, yes, the church has *a human ministry,* but there is another facet as I turn this kaleidoscopic Scripture around. The church not only has *a human ministry* (it's interested in people), but it also has . . .

A Healing Ministry

Now there are two instances of healing here. There was a man, Aeneas, who had been sick for eight years, and Simon Peter healed him. There was a woman who was deathly sick, and she died. Simon Peter went there and raised her from the dead. Now, we are well aware that Jesus performed miracles when He was on the earth. That was inherent to His ministry. Jesus came preaching, teaching, and healing, according to the Scriptures. And when Jesus returned to heaven He empowered His disciples, and before the New Testament canon was completed they authenticated the gospel which they delivered orally by the signs, wonders, and miracles in which God enabled them to participate. And they did the same kinds of divine acts that Jesus did. I believe in healing, I really do. I believe in a supernatural God. Yes, God can heal.

Many have asked me, "Preacher, do you believe God still

heals people today?" I do! I believe the God who made the body knows how to repair the body. I believe in healing. I believe God heals people in answer to prayer. Many reading this book have been miraculously healed by God. You are a testimony to the power of God and to the ministry of prayer. Of course, we believe in healing. In fact, most of us have been healed repeatedly, and the Lord did it. It works, and don't you give the doctor all the credit for that. Give Jesus most of the credit for that. When you get sick you ought to do two things. Number one, you ought to call a good competent—hopefully a Christian—doctor. Number two, you ought to pray and ask the Great Physician to come on the scene. And as you read the Scripture you will find the church had a healing ministry.

We ought to take our prayer times (Wednesday night and other occasions) more seriously than we do. We ought to take our prayer lists very, very seriously. People have enough confidence in us to bring these prayer requests to us. We ought to be serious and responsible enough to genuinely present these names to God in prayer. Anytime anybody asks me to pray, I pray right then. If somebody comes after one of the services, I pray then. A man came down and asked, "I want you to pray for me and my wife; we are having back problems." When a person has back problems, those are tough problems. Brother, if you ever have had a back problem, you recognize that those dear people are having a hard time. And I prayed and I prayed that God would touch him and his mate, and that God would supernaturally work in their lives. "More things are wrought by prayer than this world dreams of." You never know what God might do in answer to prayer.

It's not always God's will to heal. The great miracle is not the miracle of healing. In the case of Aeneas (eight years he had been bedridden), Simon Peter declared "Jesus Christ makes thee whole, arise and make your bed, and he arose immediately." But somewhere along the way Aeneas died. He died and he went on to glory. Here was Dorcas, already dead, and Simon Peter used almost the identical words Jesus did when He went into the home of the little daughter of Jairus. Jesus said, "Talitha cumi." In the original there is only one letter's difference between what Jesus spoke to the twelve-year-old girl and what Simon Peter said to the woman named Dorcas. And he spoke the word, and she came back to life. I am not sure if he did her a favor or not. I do not know if praying her back into this world was a favor or not. It was a comfort to her friends. It gave her superabundant joy, but can you imagine how it must have been to them? Paul wrote that to be "absent from the body" is to be "in the presence of the Lord."

She was up there in glory somewhere making robes for the angels; she was a seamstress. She was up there shouting around the great throne of God. Somebody tapped her on the shoulder and said, "Dorcas, I'm sorry to interrupt your rejoicing, but Peter is praying. You must go back down there." If you and I ever had a glimpse of glory for one minute, we'd never want to come back to this old world. Peter did a favor to her friends who were grieving because they missed her.

It is not always God's will to answer a prayer and to heal the sick. Sometimes God receives more glory through the experience of sickness than He does through the experience of healing. I am not sure what the situation is in individual matters on that, but I do know that the church has a healing ministry, and believers are to take seriously the responsibility to pray for the needs in the congregation.

But, now let's turn this kaleidoscopic passage a bit more. The

church not only has *a human ministry* and *a healing ministry,* but
the church of a helping hand also has . . .

A Helping Ministry

Now let's zero in for a moment on Dorcas. Glance at her in
verse 36. We are given a little bio information about Dorcas, and
it says that Dorcas was a woman who was full of good deeds,
good works, and almsdeeds which she did. You will notice down
in verse 39 the needs Dorcas helped meet. When she died and
Simon Peter showed up, the widows in the congregation brought
their coats and garments Dorcas made while she was with them.
Dorcas had a gift of sewing. Dorcas had a consecrated needle
and thread.

Now, in the New Testament there are several lists of spiritual
gifts. I personally do not believe that the list of spiritual gifts is
exhaustive. I think that they are suggestive. I believe the Holy
Spirit is sovereign. He can give a gift of any kind He wants to—at
any time.

The gift of music is not mentioned in the New Testament in
terms of being a spiritual gift. I personally am convinced, though,
that today God gives to individuals the spiritual gift of music. I
don't believe people could sing like that if God didn't anoint them
to do it. There is a difference, brother, when anointed people
sing for Jesus and people in the world sing. There is an ingredient
altogether different in that kind of music. I hear some singing that
makes me sick because it's so bad. But the music I hear around
our church brings tears to my heart because this music is so filled
with the Spirit of God. People are gifted in the ministry of music.

But in those lists, there is a little word that's mentioned in one
of them. It mentions the little word "helps." Do you remember

that, helps? And I think Dorcas had a gift of helps—sewing. She had a gift of sewing and used it to be a help and to be a blessing to other people.

And do you know what I believe? I believe that she was just as instrumental in extending the gospel of the Lord via a dedicated needle as Simon Peter was by his gifts of fiery oratory. It is wonderful for a man to have the gift of preaching. And it is blessed when people have the gift of being able to sing. You might have a gift of help. You may be able to sew, and you may be able to use that needle and thread and spread the joy of the Lord. It is not the gift that is so important. What truly counts is that you use the gift for the Lord to be a blessing to the lives of other people.

Now grasp verse 30. This woman "was full of good works and almsdeeds which she did." See, she didn't talk about it; she wasn't just filled with good words; she was filled with good works, and she did something about it. Oh, may her tribe increase! May God give to our fellowships, our congregations a multitude of believers who have those gifts of help to genuinely help other people, and to be a blessing. Oh, consecrate what you have to Jesus.

I often think about little things and how important they are. Have you ever realized how important a paper clip is? I don't know who invented the clip. Whoever he or she is, he/she must have made a fortune. But have you ever thought about a little paper clip? What would you do without them? And, yet when you look at them, there's really not a whole lot of wire. The value of the paper clip is not in the amount of wire; the value is in the bending of the clip.

That is exactly how it is in your life. It is not your gift in and of itself that is of so much value to the Lord, but it is that gift and the bend you allow the Lord to give it that makes it a boon to others. Oh, we ought to be able to help people with what God has given to us. Be a blessing. Dorcas had a gift to sew, and she used it. When she was gone people missed her, and they longed to see her again. Will anyone miss you when you are gone? Will anyone say, "Boy, I wish he hadn't died"? When you hear of the death of some people, it doesn't seem to faze you one way or the other, does it? There are many people who, if you mentioned them dying, it would break my heart. It would grieve me. They would be missed. There are certain people, and when they die, it will be good riddance so far as their influence and their impact in this world. But other people will be missed, because they have been a blessing, a help, a benefactor in this world.

The church has a helping ministry. But now then, I want to tie it all together. The church has *a human ministry*, the church has *a healing ministry*, the church has *a helping ministry,* and it has . . .

A Heavenly Ministry

At the conclusion of each one of these miracles the Lord did through Simon Peter, there is a significant statement. When Aeneas was healed in Lydda (v. 35), look at the verse, "And all that dwelt at Lydda and Saron saw him." And, what was the result? "And turned to the Lord." Some people were saved. Go to verse 42. After the miracle of the raising from the dead of Dorcas, we read in verse 42, "And it was known throughout all Joppa; and many believed in the Lord."

What were the results of it all? People got saved! It is thrilling when a person is healed physically. It's marvelous when people are helped and blessed by the ministry of sweet Christian people.

The ultimate priority and the consummate goal of all we do in a congregation of believers is to result in the salvation of precious souls and prepping people for heaven. That is the church's priority. The grandest thing that ever happens around this fellowship is when an individual, be they old or be they young, be they big or be they small, repents of their sin, receives Jesus Christ as Lord and Savior of their lives, and is born into the family of God. Heaven becomes all excited. I personally don't think heaven becomes nearly as excited about some things down here as we do. When a soul gets saved, a child is born into the family of God, and a child of the devil becomes a child of the Lord. It is "fruit basket turnover" in heaven up there. "Ring the bells of heaven, there is joy today for a soul returning from the wild."

That's what it's all about. Your greatest need is not the social ministry of a dedicated Dorcas sewing to make you a garment. Your greatest need is not a physical healing, though God may be pleased in His sovereign purpose and grace to give healing to you. But the greatest need you have in your life is to know the forgiveness of sin which comes through a personal relationship with Jesus Christ. Without Jesus Christ, you don't have anything. You may have culture; but without Christ, it's dignified paganism. You may have education; but without Jesus, it is enlightened paganism. You may have entertainment; without Jesus Christ, it is amused paganism. You may have religion; but without Jesus, it is religious paganism. What you need is to receive Jesus as your Lord and Savior.

7
Knocking Down the Wall

In Christ there is no East or West
In Him no South or North,
But one Great Fellowship of Love
Throughout the whole wide earth.
                    —John Oxenham

Acts 10:1-16

There was a certain man in Caesarea called Cornelius, a centurion of the band called the Italian band.

A devout man, and one that feared God with all his house, which gave much alms to the people and prayed to God always.

He saw in a vision evidently about the ninth hour of the day, that's 3:00 p.m., an angel of God coming into him saying unto him, Cornelius!

And when he looked on him he was afraid and said, What is it, Lord? And he said unto him, Thy prayers and thine alms are come up for a memorial before God.

Now send me to Joppa, and call for one Simon, whose surname is Peter.

He lodgeth with one Simon of tanner whose house is by the seaside. He shall tell thee what thou oughtest to do.

And when the angel which spake unto Cornelius was departed, he called two of his household servants and a devout soldier of them that waited on him continually and when he had declared all these things unto them, he sent them to Joppa.

On the morrow as they went on their journey and drew nigh unto the city, Peter went up upon the housetop to pray about the sixth hour:

And he became very hungry, and would have eaten; but while they made ready, he fell into a trance;

And saw heaven open, and a certain vessel descending unto him as it had been a great sheet knit at the four corners and let down to the earth wherein where all manner of four-footed beasts of the earth and wild beasts and creeping things and fowls of the air.

And there came a voice to him, Arise, Peter, kill and eat!

But Peter said, Not so Lord, for I have never eaten anything that is common or unclean.

And the voice spake unto him again the second time, What God hath cleansed that call not thou common.

This was done three times; and the vessel was received up again in the heavens.

This has to be one of the most pivotal chapters in the entire Word of God. The lessons taught in this chapter have made it possible for the gospel of Jesus Christ to be preached to all people everywhere, virtually to the entire human race. This particular chapter shatters prejudice in the life of the believer and opens the doors wide for Gentiles to accept Jesus Christ and have the opportunity to be saved. What took place in Acts 10 rocked the early church and actually threatened to divide it. If the events of this chapter had not taken place, chances are that the gospel of Jesus Christ would never have been brought to our shores. The substance of this chapter is vital to an understanding of the kind of gospel that Jesus Christ has given us to declare. Some people have called this the "Gentile Pentecost." Up until this point in the spread of the early church, the believers had primarily been chosen from the Jewish people. The expansion had basically been Jewish in nature.

From this point on the gospel of Jesus had an open door to go even to the Gentiles. The vast river of love that began to flow at Calvary's cross burst every dam placed in its way and overflowed its banks, reaching to all people everywhere to give them an opportunity to be saved.

Let us follow carefully the unfolding of the events in this chapter, and in so doing, show you the wonderful world-wide gospel we have to proclaim. First of all, I want us to think together as the scene opens about . . .

A Groping Centurion

This account about the centurion presents an unlikely scene. We would hardly be prepared for this scene had we not already read the Book of Acts and known what was coming at this particular time. It begins in a unique way in the city of Caesarea, on the shore of the Mediterranean Sea.

Caesarea was the dominant place of the Gentile presence in the Jewish world. Here the government of the Gentiles operated; the Romans dominated the Jewish people at that time.

The scene also begins in the barracks of a Roman army camp. The Roman Army represented the domination of that power so oppressive and so despicable to the Jewish people. It also begins in the life of Cornelius who was a military man. He was obviously well-disciplined and well-trained; a tough-minded, brave-hearted kind of man. When you read what the Scripture says about Cornelius, you are immediately aware that he was a very impressive man.

For instance, we are impressed by the *sincerity* of this man. Make note of the four statements about this man in verse 2. "He was a devout man" that "feared God with all of his house," and that he "gave much alms to the people," and "he prayed to God always." He was a Roman military man and yet the Bible presents these four positive characteristics about him. A centurion was in charge of 100 soldiers. In the New Testament, centurions come across the pages several times. For instance, you remember the centurion who had a sick servant, and he sent to Jesus and asked Him to heal the servant. And he said to Jesus, "You need not come to my house. I am not worthy that you would come under my roof." When Jesus heard these words of that centurion, Jesus explained, "I have found not so great faith in Israel." And when our Lord was dying on the cross, and when Jesus spoke the seven last words, and suffered as He did on Calvary, when the earth began to shake and the sun refused to shine, the Bible says there was a centurion standing there. He proclaimed about Jesus, "Truly this was the Son of God." And isn't it interesting that the New Testament casts a favorable light upon military men?

It seems that these tough men had open, receptive hearts to the Lord Jesus Christ. Cornelius was a very sincere man, an open man to the things of God. Yet, Cornelius was not a saved man. Would you like for me to prove it to you right out of the Scriptures? In Acts 11:14 the story is recounted of the conversion of Cornelius.

Look at verse 14: "Who shall tell thee words, [talking to the centurion] whereby thou and all thy house shall be saved." Simon Peter was to visit Cornelius's house and tell him words about how to be saved. What that means is that Cornelius in 10:2 still was not saved. It's rather startling, isn't it?

Look at the caliber of the people in the Book of Acts who came to know Jesus and were saved. For instance, we are told about an Ethiopian eunuch—a very devout man. He had made a journey of several hundred miles to worship in Jerusalem, and yet it was only when he heard the gospel of Jesus on a desert road that he was saved. And then, of course, we remember in the 9th chapter, there is the story of Saul of Tarsus, a Jewish rabbi. Only when he was stricken to the ground on the Damascus Road did he have a saving encounter with Jesus Christ. Cornelius, a devout man, Cornelius, a giving man, Cornelius, a praying man, a sincere man, but he was a lost man who needed Jesus. He was not only a *sincere* man, he was also a *searching* man. There was a hunger his heart.

He must have been tired of the politics of his empire. Probably he had grown weary with the idolatry of his day. The superstitions of the time had failed to produce any heart-satisfying results in his life, and so he was searching, groping, reaching out. His searching didn't save him, and yet God honored his searching. When a man responds to the light God has given him, God will give him even more light. His prayers went up before God as a memorial, and God dispatched an angel to tell Cornelius what to do. And so the angel came down, we are told, and in verses 3 and following, we are informed that the angel instructed Cornelius to dispatch some men to Joppa, about thirty miles away, for one named Simon Peter. Isn't it weird that the angel didn't tell him how to be saved? Have you ever wondered why the angels don't win people to Jesus? If you have accepted Jesus, guess what you're able to do. You can go with your testimony into the home or business of anyone who will open the door to you, and you can testify to them, "I was once lost like you are, and yet I realized my need for Jesus, and I asked Him to forgive me of my sin. I invited him by faith to come into my heart and into my life; and what Jesus has done for me, He will do for you." There is not an angel around the throne of God who can tell that to another human being! God has chosen to allow saved sinners to go and tell other sinners that what he has done for them, he can also do for them. And, so here we find this man, a groping centurion. But now, as the passage unfolds, we see this needy centurion, but secondly . . .

A Growing Christian

Thirty miles away there is a man named Simon Peter. We're quite familiar with him. Now I want to show you what God does. It's as if God reaches down and lays hold of the life of Cornelius, and He reaches over there and lays hold of his servant Simon Peter, and He brings these two together.

Simon Peter is a Christian, and this is after the Day of Pentecost. He has been filled on several occasions with the Spirit of God; he is the one who stood and preached with tremendous power on the Day of Penetcost. He has even raised the dead. Yet, in the Scripture pertaining to him on this occasion, you will discover that he was a Christian who still needed to grow in the Lord. There were attitudes in his heart that ought not to have been there. He had some dispositions that were not pleasing to the Lord. There was plenty of room for spiritual growth. Oh, don't get impatient with Simon Peter. Don't give up on Simon Peter. He's growing in the Lord. He's going to make it, but he must grow.

Aren't you glad God is patient with us and gives us time to grow? Have you grown any as a Christian? I surely hope you have. I know I've grown as a Christian. I'm a better Christian now than I have been. I'm closer to the Lord than I have been, and I have grown in some attitudes and in some dispositions that are helping me to be a better witness for Jesus Christ than I used to be.

God sometimes takes awhile to work in the life of His people to get some things out and to put some things in that need to be there. I want you to see how God works with a growing Christian. We know Simon Peter was an Orthodox Jew. Simon Peter was steeped in the religion of his fathers. Deeply ingrained in him was the religion of Abraham, Isaac, and Jacob. He was a rigid follower of the biblical rules. He did everything one is supposed to do. He was right down the line. But God had to change Simon Peter enough to prepare him to go over and tell Cornelius about Jesus Christ.

What did He use? One thing he used was the matter of *circumstances*. Key in on verse 6. It tells us that Simon Peter was lodging with Simon who was a tanner; whose house was by the sea. A tanner, of course, is a man who deals in animals hides. He killed animals, skinned them, and then processed their hides. It was not a pleasant work. There was an awful odor about it. You didn't want to live close to a tanner, and most Jews didn't want to get around that. Yet, there was Simon Peter staying a few days with a tanner. Before his conversion Simon probably wouldn't even have dreamed about being there. God somehow has a means of taking *circumstances* and teaching you what you need to know. God will put you in a corner sometimes, and He will force you, by the very nature of circumstances, to grow in your Christian life. That's true in my life. God has certainly done that in my own experience.

But God did something else, not only by *circumstances,* but God was also going to help Simon Peter grow by *confrontation*. Now focus on the scenario. It was about lunchtime, and Simon

Peter was up on the rooftop of the house. In those days, they had flat roofs which were for a variety of purposes, one of which was for meditation. And the Bible says he was praying about noontime. He became very hungry and he would have eaten (v. 10). I can almost imagine that. He was over the shores of the Mediterranean, maybe looking out over the sea and wondering about the people beyond the horizon, wondering what God's plan and purpose was for them.

Verse 10 says he fell into a trance. He fell into an ecstasy, and God confronted Simon Peter with a vision. In verse 11, he saw a great sheet come down out of heaven, and on that sheet (v. 12) there were all kinds of animals. In other words, "Simon, you're hungry, so I am giving you a veritable Noah's Ark to pick from. "Simon, you're hungry; I will deliver you a meat market." But there was only one problem that went with that meat market. It wasn't kosher. And so the Lord, in essence, said to Simon Peter, "All of those animals up there in that sheet are for you." And there came a voice, "Arise, Peter, kill and eat." And Simon Peter remonstrated (let me paraphrase verse 14), "Not on your life, Lord. Not me, Lord. You know me. I'm a strict Jew." That is because he was under the Old Testament laws concerning clean and unclean animals—dietary laws. To this day, Orthodox Jews would never eat pork, fish without scales like catfish and eels, and the like. Simon Peter abstained from so-called unclean meats for religious reasons.

So when the Lord said to him, "Arise, Peter, kill and eat," he replied, "Not so, Lord." Right there is a contradiction. You really cannot speak that sentence and be consistent, did you know that? "Not so, Lord." You cannot put those words in the same sentence.

Jesus Christ is Lord. He is absolute Lord. You don't make Him Lord. God made him Lord by virtue of the cross and the resurrection. God hath made Jesus Christ Lord. You don't make Him Lord; you simply yield to his Lordship. He is either Lord of all of your life, or He is not Lord at all. You are not supposed to call Him Lord and say "not so" to Him in the same verse. God was beginning to help Simon Peter to grow. You know exactly what the vision represented, don't you? And you know what the sheet and the animals represent. It represented all the nations of the world, all of the races of humanity. Simon Peter was sick to his stomach and totally repulsed. He felt better than every one of them, and so he cried to the Lord, "Not so, Lord." Notice verse 14. "For I have never," (have you ever heard those words before?) "I have never."

Ralph Neighbour, Jr. wrote a book entitled *The Seven Last Words of the Church*. Know what they are? "We've never done it that way before." "Oh, we've never done it that way. We've never tried that." We must be willing to change some methods and do some different things to reach people for the Lord. Now the message doesn't change. The Word of God is infallible, and it does not change. It is immutable and irreplaceable.

The Word doesn't change, but the methods used to convey the Word to the people who need Jesus has to change, and we have to be willing to say, "Lord, though I have never, I will if that's what You want me to do." "I have never."

And then God made a statement that absolutely shattered the prejudice in the heart of Simon Peter. The Lord said to him in verse 15, "What God hath cleansed, that call not thou common." Oh, Simon hadn't understood the far-reaching effects of the blood of Jesus at the cross. When the blood of Jesus was shed at

Calvary's cross, the Lord Jesus laid aside all the biblical dietary restrictions. When He did that, the Lord Jesus Christ made it clear that there is no such thing as a common race of people—and that the only factor that makes a person unclean is not the providence of their birth but the sin problem, and the blood of Jesus Christ cleanses from all sin. When Jesus shed his blood on the cross, he made it possible for "whosoever will" to be cleansed from their sin. There are no common people in this world.

Like Simon Peter, we need to deal with the prejudice in our hearts. Sometimes you sit down with a piece of paper, and write out those folks who would be unacceptable to you. You go home with that list and lift it into the face of God, and say, "Not so, Lord."

Every person on this earth has a right to hear the gospel of Jesus Christ. I praise God for how He has worked in our midst. I praise God for how He has worked in my life. I was born right here in the South. I came up with the same kinds of prejudices that most of us Southerners grew up with, and I can remember my attitudes and actions as a boy, and I knew in my heart they weren't right, they weren't pleasing to the Lord, but it was our culture, the society in which we lived. I remember one time I went to pastor a church, and it was made very plain to me if a person with a different color of skin should enter that church, that a large number of those people would not accept those other folks.

I was a young preacher boy, but I had read enough of my Bible to know that the Bible declares, "Whosoever will, let him come." I want to tell you something is wrong with a church that claims to preach the "whosoever-will gospel," and not allow "whosoever will" to come and hear that whosoever-will gospel.

And I remember the first time a person of another race came walking down the aisle of that church. I had already talked to my family about that, and my boys were little bitty at that time. The girls had gone on home with Janet. I think she had come to the early service, and they had gone on home; and so this person of another race came walking down the aisle of that church.

We had a counseling program like we do here, and when the service was over, my two boys climbed into the car, and they implored, "What's going to happen?"

And I answered, "What do you mean, boys?"

And they said, "Is the church going to accept this man that joined the church?"

"Well, Boys, I don't know if they will or not. I know I'm going to accept him. If anyone in the church doesn't accept him, I'm just going to resign."

"What are we going to do, Daddy?

"If you resign, where are we going?"

"Boys, I don't know where we are going," I said, "but let me tell you something, Boys: The God we serve and the God whose Bible we preach will honor you if you'll be faithful to His Word."

To make a long story short, God gave victory in that church over that situation. And I praise God that in dear old Southland of ours, though there is still prejudice in the hearts of many people, there are some churches where the color of your skin doesn't matter. It doesn't matter how much money you have in the bank; it doesn't matter how much education or lack of education you have; it doesn't make a bit of difference in the world— anybody who wants to can walk in the doors of the church and hear the saving gospel of the Lord Jesus Christ.

Sometimes I visit and folks say, "Oh, that church is too big down there." "All them folks are rich down there." And I reply, "That's a surprise to me." Did you know you folks are rich? There are folks out here who say you are. And they say, "Oh no, I couldn't come to that church down here." I reply, "Listen, friend, it doesn't matter who you are, where you live in the city of Jacksonville, what you've got on—you can walk into the church and you'll be accepted at First Baptist Church of Jacksonville." I like a church like that. I like a *people* church. I don't like a poor man's church. I don't like a rich man's church. I don't like an undereducated man's church. I don't like an educated man's church. I like a people church where "whosoever will" may come and hear the message of the Lord.

So the Lord said to Simon Peter, "What God hath cleansed, don't you call it common." We have no right to reject those whom Jesus Christ has accepted. We have no right to call common those whom God calls His children. Simon Peter was probably scratching his head about that time. That meat was sizzling down in the kitchen below. The Mediterranean Sea was stretching out in front.

About that time, there was a knock on the door. Cornelius had sent two of his servants and one soldier to call for Simon Peter. He went downstairs and said, "Yes. I know what you're talking about. Spend the night with us, and tomorrow we'll take off." The next day Simon Peter enlisted some men to go with him, and he headed out to Caesarea. Now that brings me to the third point I want you to see.

A Gathering Centurion

During this time, Cornelius has been doing some work. He's been gathering friends. And he's been gathering his family to-

gether. And he explained to them, "We've got a preacher who is
going to come, and we're going to have a house service. And this
preacher is going to give us some words that will tell us about
salvation."

So when Simon Peter arrived at Cornelius's house, (notice
what it says in verse 33 the middle of the verse): "Now, therefore,
they say to Simon Peter, are we all here present before God to
hear all things that are commanded thee of God?" That was an
ideal congregation. Did you know the congregation has a strong
influence on the message? There is an electric spark that occurs
between preacher and pulpit when all systems are go for Christ.
Now, the young people are really expressive when the preacher
is in tune, and when the congregation is responding and receptive, they put it like this: "Preacher, you were cooking this morning." That's a pretty good way to describe it. People can make a
message or kill a message by your response. This is how we
ought to attend every service. When folks are in that kind of attitude, that is the greatest sort of preaching situation anywhere—
people who want to hear the Word of God, people who have a
hunger for God's truth. God surely is pleased with a church like
that. God becomes interested and He will send His Word to people who have a thirst for the Word of God.

Some churches don't have the Word because they don't want
the Word. The prophet Amos said one time there would be a
famine of the hearing of the Word of God. You know why he
prophesied that? Because the people didn't want to hear the
Word of God. But where there is eagerness in the hearts of people to hear the Word, they'll hear it. Starting at verse 34 and
reading right through the chapter, you will discover that to that
gathering congregation he preached a sermon about a *universal*

Savior and a *universal salvation*. And he said in verse 34, "Of a truth I perceive that God is no respecter of persons." The point was: "I know that our God loves every person everywhere." Jesus is not just a black man's Savior. Not just a white man's Lord. Not just a yellow man's Redeemer. Jesus is every man's potential Lord and Savior. "Red and yellow, black and white, they are precious in His sight." Recently two fine young men in our church gave their testimonies—one a white man and one, a black. I couldn't tell any difference, could you? They had on different ties, but isn't it wonderful that God is no respecter of persons?

Deal with that in your life. If you have any vestiges of your old prejudice, you had better ask God to purge it. You can't be an effective witness for the Lord if there is ugly prejudice, bigotry, hatred, and animosity in your heart. Accept what God says, "God is no respecter of persons." Peter, who struggled with prejudice against Gentiles, preached a universal Savior and a universal salvation. "Whosoever will can be saved."

Verse 43 is thrilling. Here's the simple plan—"To him give all the prophets witness that through his name . . ." Praise God for this word. "Whosoever believeth in Him shall receive remission of sins." That means, regardless of the color of your skin, regardless of what your economic situation may be, anybody who wants to be saved can be saved! That was good preaching, Simon.

He was about through with his second point and getting ready for his third, and he stopped the sermon. Verse 44: "While Peter yet spake these words"—he wasn't through. "While Peter yet spake these words, the Holy Spirit fell on all them that heard the word . . ." Then on to verse 45: "And they of the circumcision which believed were astonished." The Jews present did not believe such could happen. "As many as came with Peter because that on the Gentiles also was poured the gift of the Holy Ghost. For they heard them speak with tongues" [same thing that happened at Pentecost] (v. 45*b*). I do not believe tongues entered into their salvation. They were a sign gift, still in operation at that time. They spoke with tongues, and they magnified God. At that very moment, they were saved. "You mean, Preacher, they didn't go to the counseling room? You mean they didn't come forward in the invitation?" "Well, what does it say?" "While Peter yet spake the Spirit fell." And on the Gentiles was poured out the gift of the Holy Spirit.

My copastor Dr. Lindsey told me the other Tuesday, "Boy, I've got a real visit tonight. These folks been watching on television, and they have called up, wanting to be saved. I'm going over there." I offered: "I'd be glad to take that card for you." He is the most selfish pastor with his prospect cards you ever saw. He hides them! No, no, no, he wouldn't let me have that card. Well, when he got there, they had already been saved. Ha, ha, ha. Wouldn't you like to see the power of God become so real in your church and mine that sometime before we get through preaching the sermon, folks start coming down the aisle yelling, "What must I do to be saved?"

I remember one time I was preaching in Mobile (and this was right in the hippie era). During the sermon, a hippie girl jumped up from her seat and ran down to the front, and fell right there on her knees. We stopped everything and won her to the Lord right then and there. It doesn't matter whether I finish the sermon or not. The whole point of the sermon is to reach people for Jesus. We are not preaching just to deliver pretty sermons. We're preaching for souls to be saved.

Now what's the next step? New Testament evangelism. Here is New Testament evangelism, verse 47, last sentence. Then answered Peter, "Can any man forbid water? That these should not be baptized which have received the Holy Spirit as well as we?" And the chapter ends with, "And he commanded them to be baptized in the name of the Lord" (v. 48). The New Testament pattern is this. Make disciples; baptize them. I become a little bit suspicious about the folks who see so many people saved and yet they never show up at church. They never walk down the church aisle and are never baptized.

You haven't done it the New Testament way until you do it exactly as it was done in the house of Cornelius. Cornelius was saved, and they led him to the water. Ditto for his household.

Baptism doesn't save. Oh, no. Peter could have said, "Be circumcised." That would have linked them with the old dispensation and the Jews. But Peter said, "Be baptized." That linked them with the new dispensation and with Jesus. Baptism does not save, but it confirms salvation. It is an outward demonstration of an inward transformation that has taken place in your heart. If you will invite Jesus to come into your heart, He will—and He will save you and forgive you of your sins. Then you can be an obedient believer and follow the Lord in baptism, and begin growing in the Lord.

8
Christians!

The spirit of the early Christians was contagious. While they were in prayer meetings, and while they were reading their Scriptures, and while they were gathered together, they were preparing to go out and permeate the world. . . . those who once looked on them in ridicule and criticism were bearing the same faith before long . . .

—Bailey E. Smith

Acts 11:19-30

Now they which were scattered abroad upon the persecution that arose about Stephen traveled as far as Phoenicia and Cyprus and Antioch, preaching the word to none but unto the Jews only.

And some of them were men of Cyprus and Cyrene which when they were come Antioch, spake unto the Greek preaching the Lord Jesus.

And the hand of the Lord was with them, and a great number believed and turned unto the Lord.

Then tidings of these things came unto the ears of the church which was in Jerusalem. And they sent forth Barnabas that he should go as far as Antioch.

Who, when he came and had seen the grace of God, was glad, and exhorted them all that with purpose of heart they would cleave unto the Lord.

For he was a good man and full of the Holy Spirit and of faith. And much people was added onto the Lord.

Then departed Barnabas to Tarsus for to seek Saul.

And when he had found him, he brought him unto Antioch. And it came to pass that a whole year they assembled themselves with the church and taught much people, and the disciples were called Christians first in Antioch.

And in those days came prophets from Jerusalem unto Antioch.

And there stood up one of them named Agabus and signified by the Spirit that there should be a great famine throughout all the world, which came to pass in the days of Claudius Caesar.

Then the disciples, every man according to his ability, determined to send relief unto the brethren which dwelt in Judea.

Which also they did and sent it to the elders by the hands of Barnabas and Saul.

In verse 27 is the first occasion in all of the Bible where believers in the Lord Jesus were called Christians. In Antioch of Syria the disciples of Jesus were called Christians for the first time. The word "Christian" really means "one who belongs to Jesus Christ," actually a copy of Christ. Aren't we to let the Holy Spirit make us more like the Master. Now, the term Christian was not given by the Christians to describe themselves, but rather it was a term that was used by the people in Antioch to describe the kind of conduct and the life-style which they saw demonstrated by the believers in the Lord. It was actually kind of a word used in scorn, in ridicule. It was a term of rebuke. Yet, as is so often true, the Lord employed a word intended to be an insult, and turned it into the most popular appellation ever applied to those who are followers of Christ. Those who know Christ are all too glad to be identified as Christians, those who belong to Jesus.

I want to continue our consideration of what it means to be a

Christian. When the people in Antioch coined this term, they used it in its plural form. Look again at verse 26, the last sentence. "And the disciples [plural] were called Christians [plural] first in Antioch." The disciples were called Christians. When individuals came to know Christ and were saved, they became a part of what we refer to as the church of the Lord Jesus. There is the church invisible, the body of Christ, where every person who knows Jesus as Savior is a member. There is also the church visible, that local manifestation of the body of Christ in a city, in a village, in a country somewhere when God's people gather together and call themselves Christians. What are the elements that make a church a "Christian" congregation? What gives a church a right to call itself a "Christian" church, a group of believers who gather themselves together and are called Christians?

I believe that the need of every area is a church that is indeed a Christian church, not a Christian merely as a title but Christian in truth. I am talking about a body of believers who are so much like the Lord Jesus that the people in that place can tell those people have been with Jesus. That's the kind of church that will make an impact on a city for the Lord Jesus Christ.

I believe it's possible to take a city for Jesus. I am not making the claim that every individual in a place can be won to Christ, but I do believe it is possible for a church to be so Christian—to be so much like the Lord—that it has an eternal influence on that city for the Lord. The Lord intends for a church to be like salt in a city, preserving it from corruption. He also intends a Christian church to be like light in that city, dispelling the darkness of despair.

Now, I want to point out this: A church is Christian when it is made up of . . .

A Converted People

The account of how these people came to Christ in Antioch is one of the most fantastic stories in all of the Bible. Here was a city with a population of approximately a half million people, the third largest city in the Roman Empire. It was known for its extreme immorality—a city of sports gone mad, of chariot racing, loose living, and orgies. Into this city the gospel of Jesus Christ was carried, and many were converted and then came to be called Christians. What were the elements that resulted in the conversion of these people? Now, I want to touch on the conversation of the believers. "Now they which were scattered abroad" (v. 19). This verse has almost the same terminology that is used in Acts 8:4. In a real sense, this ties directly into Acts 8:4, which states, "Therefore, they that were scattered abroad went everywhere preaching the word." Tying directly to that is 11:19 that goes, "Now, they which were scattered abroad . . ." —same group of people, same individuals, believers from the city of Jerusalem carrying the good news of Christ to the city of Antioch.

They were preaching the Word. Now the word "preaching" there does not mean the kind of preaching I do. It was not the public proclamation of the gospel that we do in our public services. There are several words translated as preaching in the New Testament. One of the words is one that means "public proclamation," "declaring the Word of God," "announcing the good news of the gospel." The word used here is a different one, a word that could be translated "evangelizing the gospel." That word pictures what we would call "life-style evangelism," conversational evangelism. It doesn't mean they were having revival meetings and crusades. What it means is that everywhere those disciples went, they were talking about Jesus.

God has given us a method of shaping the country, the villages, the towns, and the cities for Jesus. That method is the personal witness of those who claim Jesus as their Savior. It is God's method. There are many ways to win people. We have the media of television and radio. At our church we televise our Sunday morning service, and we are on four hours every week. And there are billboards and the print media. Thank God for every person who comes to know Jesus that way. People come to know Christ as a result of our public services, but Jesus, when He wanted the Christians to get down to business to win a city to the Lord, gave us the pattern.

We are to team up two by two and to go out into "the highways and hedges" and tell people one on one about Jesus. There is no better method than that. It is not that the method of public witnessing has been tried and found wanting, but rather that it has been tried and found difficult. God intends for his people to share the good news of Jesus everywhere they go talking to people about the Lord. Through the testimonies of our young people we have a multitude who are witnessing for Jesus on their high school campuses. Some of them have claimed their high school for the Lord. One of our teenage girls claimed her high school for the Lord, and she decided to start at the top. She marched herself right into the principal's office and witnessed to her. It happened that the principal was a Christian and thanked her for coming in to tell her about Jesus.

Now, what would happen if all of us who work in businesses in our areas would start taking that approach? What if we kind of claimed our places of work for the Lord. I mean make up a prayer list and start praying for the people around us who need Jesus as their personal Savior. One of our men told me what a change had happened to a man who worked with him. The fellow happened to work in a post office. He was saved, and as he came to work, everybody in that post office knew that he had been saved. When I heard that I thought about another post office in Oklahoma. Do you remember how a man walked in with a gun, and before he was finished had killed fifteen people and put a bullet in his own head. I started praying, "Lord, what if there had been a soul-winner in that post office? Suppose there had been a soul-winner who had gotten a burden on his heart for that deranged man who had problems and needed to know Jesus. And suppose instead of that guy walking in with a revolver, he had gone in and announced, "Hey, everybody! I got saved and Jesus has given me a reason to live and has put a love in my heart." Do you see the difference a soul-winner can mean in a place?

And so the early believers went everywhere telling folks about Jesus. Verse 19 indicates that some spoke the word only to Jews. Verse 20 points out that some of them started speaking to the Greeks about the Lord Jesus. I guess they figured, "Well, if it's good enough for the Jews, it's sure good enough for the Greeks. They must have reasoned, *If Jesus saves Jews, then why wouldn't Jesus save anybody? And if Jesus would die on the cross for Jews, why couldn't Jesus die for the whole world*—and He did! There is no one beyond the scope of the love of Jesus. Every person deserves to hear about Jesus. So there was witnessing, the conversational evangelism of these people. I like verse 21: "And the hand of the Lord was with them." When you get interested in what God is interested in, then God will get interested in what you are interested in. If you want to have the constant presence of God in your life, get in the work of God— God's business. Have you ever felt the hand of the Lord upon your life? I pray so. I have felt God's hand while I was preaching. Sometimes while I have been preaching, it seemed as if the hand of the Lord came down and touched me. The psalmist sang: "Thou has laid thy hand upon me."

I think about a wedding reception. The bride and the groom are usually radiant. And she's ready to cut the cake, and that groom of hers puts his hand on top of her hand and he helps her cut that cake. When you start cutting the cake for God, He puts His hand on your hand.

I have felt God's presence in this pulpit while I have preached. I have sensed the hand of God on my life while on my knees in prayer, but where have I sensed the hand of God upon my life more than any other place? It's when I go into a home and take the Scripture, and step by step I begin to introduce those people to the way of salvation. I have felt the presence of God so real and the power of God so strong in homes where I have shared Jesus. It's as though Jesus Himself were in that room with you, and He was! And He is. You want the presence of God to be real in your life; get in the soul-winning business. I am like most Christians. There are visitation nights when, to be perfectly honest, I don't feel much like it.

Isn't it amazing what a defeat in football can do for people's spiritual life? It helps you understand where your joy is. Either you find your supreme joy is in Jesus or something else. In fact, one of our deacons and I were rejoicing in the goodness of God yesterday, praising God for His goodness, and one of our men had the nerve to remark, "It's time to get down to spiritual things. We ain't got time to talk about that." I had never heard him that

CHRISTIANS! **139**

interested in spiritual things before. I don't go soul-winning because I feel like going soul-winning. I want you to know if you're going to be a soul-winner on the basis of your emotions, the devil will send you enough indigestion to keep you from being one. I'm a soul-winner because God in His Word instructed me to be one. I've gone out in my car and felt nothing. The presence of God was not at all real in me, as far as I could tell. Some of those nights when I have not been "in season," but went soul-winning anyhow, a wonderful sense of the presence of God flooded that place. Then when the people you do visit fall on their knees, the tears come, and the prayer is lifted to heaven, and you see them weep their way into the family of God. The hand of God becomes powerful upon you. And you go home rejoicing.

They witnessed the hand of the Lord on them, and a great number believed, and turned unto the Lord (v. 21). When is a church Christian?—when it is truly a *converted church*. These were people who gave evidence of being converted. They had believed and they had turned to the Lord. May we be a Christian church.

Number two, a church is a Christian church when there is . . .

A Charming People

Now, let me explain what I mean. When the word was received in Jerusalem, the mother church, that God was doing a work in Antioch, they decided they had better send an emissary to check out the situation. There was one obvious choice, our old friend, Brother Barnabas. I mean Barnabas, the son of encouragement, the man who was willing to give people a second chance. Verse 24: "He was a good man, and full of the Holy Ghost and of faith."

When Barnabas arrived in Antioch, he saw grace. Verse 23:

"Who when he came and had seen the grace of God . . ." That is a strange statement. He had seen the grace of God. Wait a minute. How can you see grace? Grace is a spiritual intangible—you can't see grace. A young fellow said, "Uh-huh, yeah, you can see Grace. She is 5'2", weighs 110 pounds, has blonde hair and blue eyes." No, grace is a spiritual intangible. There's a verse (Mark 2:5) that helps us at this point. This passage will throw additional light on chapter 11. This is the Scripture where four men brought a man who was sick of the palsy to Jesus. They couldn't go inside the house, because the people were crammed in there to hear Jesus. So they climbed up on the roof, tore the roof up, and then lowered the man right down into the presence of Jesus. Mark 2:5: "And when Jesus saw their faith . . ." Faith, like grace is a spiritual intangible. What does it mean "when Jesus saw their faith?" It means that Jesus saw the effects of their faith. He recognized what faith produced in their lives.

Now, back to Acts 11. Verse 23 records that Barnabas "saw grace in their lives." Have you ever seen grace in a life? Surely I have. You have seen the effects of grace in the life of a person. I remember John West of Rome, Georgia. When I was pastor there many years ago, after a series of elections and referendums—we won several of them—but finally after some trickery in the state legislature—actually some manipulation—the wet forces were able to disenfranchise the county that was dry, and they legalized liquor in the city. The first person to apply for a liquor license was John West. John West had been visiting the church where I was pastor. So, I immediately made a visit to John's house. "John, I've come over here to plead with you to withdraw that application for that license. You don't need to do that. God is not pleased with it. John, what you need is Jesus. And you need to be saved, John."

John wouldn't listen to me, his wife became incensed, and they virtually kicked me out of the house. And I showed them where God puts a curse on people who give strong drink to their neighbor. God has a rule for those who entice people to drink. I showed that passage as lovingly and as tactfully as I knew how— it didn't do any good. He was given the first liquor license, and within a distance of two or three blocks from our church, just outside the legal distance, he built a building and put in the first liquor store in our city. It broke my heart.

To make a long story short, one day God grabbed hold of John West. And I *saw* God come into the life of John West. He sold the liquor store. The day came that John West walked down the aisle of that church and gave his public testimony. I baptized him, and I began to *see* grace in his life. And I *saw* the grace of God all over. There's the solution—the liquor dealer just needs Jesus. That's the whole solution—lead him to Jesus. Get him hooked on the power of the man of Galilee. That will solve his problem. And I *saw* God work, I *saw* grace.

You can see grace in a life. You can also see sin in a life. Did you know you can see the effects of sin in a life? If you will only look at the differences between the saint and the sinner, I believe a reasonable mind would be compelled to receive Jesus as Lord and Savior now. You can see the grace of God.

You can see the grace of God in a church. I can tell when grace is at work in a church. I can tell it by the Bibles that are open, by the kind of singing that's going on, by the tears in the eyes, and the fellowship there. I can surely tell it when people start making decisions for Christ. And there was . . .

A Caring People

God's grace works in a life, and you can see it. Barnabas was sensitive enough to see grace in the life of an individual. I want you to notice another fact—he encouraged growth.

In verse 23 it says, "And he was glad." He was glad and exhorted them all that with purpose of heart they would cleave unto the Lord." Barnabas epitomized the caring of Christians. Barnabas was an encourager, not a discourager. I want to be an encourager, don't you? Hadn't you rather be an encourager than a discourager? Oh, don't be a discourager. Don't be an inspector of warts and a collector of carbuncles. Don't run a sewage department. You ought to wonder about sour people. They look like they were born in the subjunctive mood and weaned on a dill pickle. Every time you see them, God is blessing the church, folks are being saved, but it just looks like they are miserable and unhappy. I pray, "Dear Lord, help me, help me to grow sweeter and sweeter and sweeter, and to be an encourager to people."

He exhorted them to cleave unto the Lord. "I want you to grow," he was urging them. See, grace not only saves you, but grace makes you grow. The Bible says, "Of his fullness, have all we received, and grace for grace" (John 1:16). You can grow in grace. In 2 Peter 3:18 it says, "Grow in grace, and in the knowledge of our Lord and Saviour, Jesus Christ." Barnabas encouraged growth, but he also provided guidance. Then he realized that the church needed more than he was able to give them. They needed unconditional ministry. They needed someone with gifts he didn't have in order to fully develop them in God's way. So verse 25 says, "Then departed Barnabas to Tarsus, for to seek Saul." He found him. Verse 26: "And when he had found him" conveys the idea that he had difficulty finding him. When he found him he must have asked, "Saul, where in the world have you been? God has a work of grace going on over there in Antioch, and we need a good Bible teacher. These folks need to grow in the Lord, and you're exactly the man for the job. Why don't you join me, Saul? Why don't you and I make up a team together and let's go back to that young church and provide guidance for those people?" And you know what? That's what they did. For a whole year they assembled themselves with the church and taught much people. A worthy service is to help a young Christian grow in the Lord and involve him in the growth program of a Bible-teaching local fellowship.

God never intended you just to feed on the Word and get fat and sassy—then come wobbling in on Sunday mornings and say, "Well, just coming in feeding on the Word." Oh no. You have missed the whole point of the teachings of the Scriptures, if what you are learning about the Lord makes you self-satisfied and does not produce a burning desire for you to go out and tell people about Jesus. What difference does it make whether you know the color of the beast of the Book of Revelation if souls in your community are dying minus Jesus? What's the point in being able to name from memory all of the dispensations of the Bible and not be able to name the addresses of lost people in your city.

Brother, there is plenty wrong with Bible study that only makes people haughty and arrogant Christians. Bible study will make you humble if you do it right. New Christians need to join a church where the preacher(s) is preaching and teaching the Word of God. It's how to grow as a Christian. Sit under the teaching of the Word of God. When is a church Christian? *When it's a converted* church, *when it's a charming church,* when God's grace is at work in it. Then number four, *when it's . . .*

A Concerned People

Then there came some prophets from the church in Jerusalem (v. 27). One of them was Agabus (v. 28). He stood up and he "signified by the Spirit there would be a great famine throughout all the world." And the last sentence says, "which came to pass." Exactly what he predicted would happen.

Today in the sense in which these prophets are mentioned in the Scriptures, we do not have such prophets. We have prophets in the sense that men stand in the pulpit and preach the Word of God. In those days, they did not have the completed Word of God, and so God gifted men with the ability to receive direct revelation from heaven to mediate the revelation to people. And they were able to predict the future. See, I have no need to predict the future. God has given us a book that predicts the future. I can find out all about the future in the Word of God. God has given it to us in the Word. Agabus's prediction came to pass.

The brethren heard about it in Antioch, and they determined (v. 29) to send relief to the brethren who dwelt in Judea. Here was a group of Greeks, Gentiles if you please, who had been saved by the grace of God. They were a concerned church—*a converted people, a charming people, a caring people.* And they started sending relief back to the mother church at Jerusalem. And there were some Jews in the mother church who didn't even think those Antiochan Gentiles could be saved? Can you imagine what may have happened when a big package of food came to the church in Jerusalem? The Jerusalem Christians were going through famine and destitution. Someone said, "My,

CHRISTIANS! **145**

my, look at this food. Thank God! Where did this come from?"

"Oh, it came from the church up there in Antioch—from those Gentiles!" Do you *see* what love does? Do you *see* how love reaches out to those in need, regardless of the circumstances? That's when a church is really Christian. It's when a church has a heart of love that flows out to people who have needs (and all of us do). This church not only sent food to the hungry, it sent its preachers out to proclaim the Word of God; and may we not only be Christians individually, may we be Christians as a church. May it be evident that everywhere we go, we belong to Jesus Christ!

9
Household Religion

There was a little home where grief and care
Had bred but courage, love, and valiant will,
I sought—and found Him there.
                                        —Anne Marriott

Acts 18:1-3,18-19,24-28

And after these things, Paul departed from Athens and came
to Corinth and found a certain Jew named Aquila born in Pontus, lately come from Italy, with his wife Priscilla; (because that
Claudius had commanded all Jews to depart from Rome;) and
came unto them. And because he was of the same craft, he
abode with them and wrought; for by their occupation they were
tent makers.

And Paul after this tarried there yet a good while, and then
took his leave of the brethren, and sailed thence into Syria, and
with him Priscilla and Aquila; having shorn his head in Cenchrea
for he had a vow. And he came to Ephesus, and left them there;
but he himself entered into the synagogue, and reasoned with
the Jews.

And a certain Jew named Apollos, born in Alexandria, an eloquent man, and mighty in the scriptures, came to Ephesus. This

man was instructed in the way of the Lord; and being fervent in the spirit, he spake and taught diligently the things of the Lord, knowing only the baptism of John. And he began to speak boldly in the synagogue; whom when Aquila and Priscilla had heard, they took him unto them, and expounded unto him the way of God more perfectly. And when he was disposed to pass into Achaia, the brethren wrote, exhorting the disciples to receive him; who, when he was come, helped them much which had believed through grace; for he mightily convinced the Jews, and that publicly, showing by the scriptures that Jesus was Christ.

Let us look in on a lovely Bible family. I am referring to the family of Aquila and Priscilla. The Bible teaches that the Christian faith is intended to be a family affair. This couple comprised . . .

A Christian Household

In Acts 16, when Paul preached the gospel to the Philippian jailer, the jailer inquired, "What must we do to be saved?" The Lord spoke through Paul, "Believe on the Lord Jesus Christ, and thou shalt be saved, and thy house."

God intends the Christian faith to be a family situation. You may remember when the Lord cast the demons out of Legion, and the Lord told Legion, "Legion, go home to thy friends and tell them what good things the Lord hath done for thee."

I have come to the conclusion that if you do not live the Christian life in the home, then probably you really don't live it anywhere else. God intends that the Christian faith make an impact on the family unit. I believe if Christians will live with Christlikeness in the family, it will result in the salvation of many unsaved family members and will be a tremendous testimony for the Lord in the community.

There are many wonderful families in the Bible. We remember, of course, the family of Mary and Joseph. Into this family the Heavenly Father sent His Son, the Lord Jesus. In that family Jesus grew in wisdom, in stature, in favor with God and man (see Luke 2:52). And then who could forget the family of Mary, Martha, and Lazarus? Their home seemed to be one of Jesus' favorite places—a little home in Bethany where Jesus could go and feel perfectly at home. Of course, there was the family of Cornelius. Cornelius, you'll remember, invited all of his friends to his house one day. Simon Peter came, preached the gospel to them, and many, many people found Jesus as their Savior.

There are lessons here about household religion in the family of Aquila and Priscilla. They are mentioned three times in Acts 18, and three other times in the Bible: Romans 16, 1 Corinthians 16, and then in 2 Timothy 4. When you put all of these passages together, you discover a touching picture of household religion, faith that is a family affair.

I want us to notice the family of Aquila and Priscilla. They had a Christian household. You can piece the accounts of this family together and gather an idea of how this couple came to know the Lord. We seem to have indications from the Bible, and from outside sources, that their family was a prominent family.

The name Aquila was a Jewish name; the name Priscilla or Priska, as it is called in some places, was a Roman name. We are not sure, but it seems that Priscilla was the more prominent of the two.

In some passages her name is mentioned first. Some Bible teachers believe that this means she was born into a family of nobility in the Roman empire. It also may indicate she was strong in spiritual matters, that she had a greater capacity for spiritual things than her husband did. I might reconstruct the story for you, using some of the traditions from history books, as well as from the Bible. It may be that Priscilla was a debutante in an influential Roman family. She met this young Jewish man, Aquila, fell in love with him, and they married.

Because of the intense spirit of anti-Semitism, which was abroad in the empire at that time, it's altogether possible that they became outcasts because of their marriage. Now, of course, there is a fact that needs to be underscored, and it is this—that all young people need to be aware of the reality that when you marry a boy or a girl, you don't merely marry them, you marry the whole family. You marry the *whole* family. The Bible teaches that a believer is only to marry another believer. In 2 Corinthians 6:14 the Bible emphasizes very plainly, "Be not unequally yoked together with unbelievers." That could not be more explicit. And then in 1 Corinthians 7:39, it's talking about widows who are preparing to marry again and Paul basically says to them (paraphrasing), "You're free to marry anybody you want to" (and then he added this statement): "Only in the Lord." Young people, if you'll make up your mind to marry only a Christian boy or girl, you will be obedient to the Word, and God will bless you.

Several years ago where I was pastor, one of the young girls in our church was preparing to marry. The boy she wanted to marry was not a Christian. She and the boy came to me, and the boy was not interested in Jesus. I witnessed to him. He was rather obnoxious about his rejection of the Christian faith and couldn't have cared less. I said to the girl, "I'm sorry. I'm not going to marry you to this non-Christian boy." She and her whole family became furious with me. She went ahead and married the boy. They had a child. Some years later they divorced. I returned to that church years later. One night in a revival meeting this girl stood up, and she said, "Our pastor when he was here wouldn't marry me to the boy I married because he wasn't a Christian." She continued, "I got mad at him, I was upset, I was offended by him, but I want to tell all you girls tonight, he was exactly right. I wish I had followed the direction and the spiritual guidance of my pastor."

Let me relate another story. I was preaching one night, and I made the statement that one had better marry a believer, and I said, "Now, if you're going to marry an unbeliever, don't come to me. I'm not going to marry you." Sitting in that congregation was a girl who was dating a lost boy, about to get engaged to him. And she sat there and thought to herself, *Well, my goodness, my pastor's not going to marry me if I get married to this boy*. And so she started praying for and witnessing to him. She led him to Jesus, brought him to me, I married them, and she said to me, "I've always been glad you told me what the Bible said, and I was willing to obey the Scriptures."

Young people will never go wrong doing what God commands in the Bible. Obey the Bible, and you'll always come out on top.

Aquila and Priscilla were a prominent family. But it seems also that their family was a problem family.

We know this because of what we read in the parenthesis in verse 2 of this chapter. Did you see what it says there? It says, "because that Claudius [that is, the Roman emperor] had commanded all Jews to depart from Rome." Because of that they had come from Italy into Achaia and the city of Corinth.

The emperor Claudius had determined that he was going to restore the ancient religions of the Roman empire. He hated all foreign religions, especially Judaism. So there was a period of time when there was tremendous persecution unleashed against the Jews. During this time the household of Aquila and Priscilla was uprooted, and they had to move from Italy.

It is always an upsetting and turbulent experience when you have to be picked up from where you are and move elsewhere.

I remember toward the end of World War II, my father was stationed down in St. Petersburg, Florida. I was in the second grade when my dad sent for mother and me to come down to St. Pete. I well remember my last day at school in Georgia. I felt awful saying good-bye to my friends.

And then I remember *very* well my first day at a strange school. That can absolutely be a petrifying experience—to walk into a school where you've never been before. Every eye is on you. You gaze into strange faces. That's what Aquila, Priscilla, and their family had to do.

They had a problem because of persecution which forced them to leave their home. Their problem is an illustration to us that families have all kinds of problems. That's certainly true in our day. I've never known a time when there is more pressure exerted on the family than now. Economic pressure—the pressures of trying to make ends meet. The pressures that go along with materialism, prosperity, and affluence bring special problems into the family. There are problems of immorality and the influence of a godless society on a Christian family. There is no family that does not know what it is to face the pressures brought about because of the pagan society in which we live.

If mothers and fathers are trying to rear their children in the nurture and admonition of the Lord in this kind of atmosphere, they have decided they are going to do it the hard way. Now the easy "out" for a parent is to just kind of go along—kind of "go with the flow." Let me read an article I cut out of the newspaper several weeks ago. It went: "If your 14-year-old daughter is now a high school freshman, by the time she's a senior here are the things you can expect. Two-thirds of the kids in her class will have used an illicit drug. One in five in her class will be a problem drinker. Two in five will consume five or more drinks in one sitting. Twenty percent of her classmates will smoke tobacco daily. Almost half, 46 percent, of the babies born to unmarried mothers are born to teenagers, young girls just like your daughter. One-third of all U.S. abortions are performed on teenagers, girls as young as your 14-year-old daughter. Nearly half of today's teenagers are sexually active. Intercourse begins on average at age 15 or younger. Again, often under the influence of alcohol or drugs. Two-thirds of sexually active girls do not use birth control. Every year, 30,000 girls under the age of 15 (your daughter's age, or younger), become pregnant. Maternal mortality for girls that young is two-and-a-half times greater than for women in their 40s. One-fourth of the deaths, two-fifths of the injuries that result from physical abuse, occur among teenagers. Some 600,000 teenage girls, 300,000 teenage boys worked as prostitutes. Their average age is 15, a year older than your girl is now. Drugs and alcohol play a part in that, too."

Each year, 5,000 teenagers commit suicide; 50,000 attempt it. We need a revival of real Christianity in the home. Our young people deserve to have a mama and a daddy who believe the Bible, a home where Jesus is loved, where church attendance is made an important matter.

Aquila and Priscilla, a family where there were problems, uprooted from their home, forced to move to another place. But this family was a provident family.

God was even working in the turmoil; God was behind the scenes in the move they were experiencing in order to bring something marvelous into their lives. As they were moving east, there was a man named Paul who was moving west, and when both parties arrived in the city of Corinth, they met face-to-face. It was the beginning of the most thrilling experience that ever happened in their lives.

You know that Paul was not only a preacher, but also a tent maker. What a stroke of providence—not coincidence. And we know that Aquila and Priscilla were also tent makers by occupation. And so they were drawn together by this common occupation.

Can you imagine what must have taken place? They would sit in that work room together, and Paul, with those large shears, would be cutting through that goat skin, preparing to make tents. And he talked to them about Jesus who had been born in a little place in Palestine called Bethlehem. And he would tell them about the fact that this Jesus never sinned; that this Jesus died on the cross for the sins of the whole wide world. Aquila and Priscilla had never heard such an amazing story in all their lives. The Lord used this providential affair to put them in touch with a man who could tell them how they could be saved. They were gloriously converted because they met this man named Paul. Isn't it wonderful how God does that? They moved to a place they never dreamed they would live. Do you remember moving and how you might have argued about it? You said, where? And your daddy said, "My gracious alive."

You said, "Dad, don't take us there. They tell me it's cold (hot) there all the time. Don't make us move, please."

And he said, "Well, I'm sorry, that's just where my job's moved me, and we're going there to live." So you moved to another town, next door to some strange neighbors. They were just different. When Sunday came, you'd notice along about 8 or 9:00 in the morning, they'd all walk out dressed up and with Bibles. They would be gone for two or three hours, and then come back. You wondered what in the world they were doing out that early on a Sunday morning. Then one day the doorbell rang at your house and you opened the door, and you saw a brand-new face and met a brand-new friend who presented a brand-new story about the Lord Jesus Christ, and your lives have never again been the same because of the providence of God that moved you to that situation.

It is wonderful how God works. By the way, believers ought always to be on the lookout for folks moving to a town.

Let me share a true story with you. I was speaking for Charles Billingsley's father, Brother Billingsley, some time ago at the Full-Time Evangelists' Meeting in Florida. One of those evangelists who lives here in Jacksonville talked with me: "Let me tell you what happened. I went to the dry cleaner the other day." And he said, "There was a new lady working at the counter. I went in with my dry cleaning, and I saw her. I started witnessing about the Lord, and before I could get finished she asked me, 'Do you belong to First Baptist Church?'" And he replied, "Well, no, I don't belong to First Baptist Church."

She answered, "Well, I wondered. This is my first day on the job, and you are the seventh person that's walked into this place today and witnessed to me, and the first six were members of

First Baptist Church of Jacksonville." What a tribute to our church or any church! There are people who move into your community by the providence of God, so you and I can tell them about Jesus Christ. Aquila and Priscilla had a Christian household because of God's providence.

I believe every young person has the right to a Christian family, to have a mama and daddy who love Jesus and will bring their kids up in the nurture and in the admonition of the Lord.

Not only did Priscilla and Aquila have a Christian household, but it was . . .

A Concerned Household

Every indication about Aquila and Priscilla leads us to believe they were a concerned family. Read Romans 16:3: "Greet Priscilla and Aquila, my helpers in Christ Jesus." Keep your place there and return to Acts 18. "My helpers in Christ Jesus."

We know they were fellow workers in making tents. But after they accepted Christ, they became "my helpers in Christ Jesus." What happened to them is what happens to every Christian. After you're saved, regardless of what your business may be, your main business will be to work for Jesus Christ. That's your first primary responsibility.

You explain, "Well, I sell insurance for a living." You may sell insurance for a living, but if you're a born-again child of God, you ought to be trying to win people to Jesus as your main occupation. Selling insurance is simply paying the bills and putting food on the table.

So, Aquila and Priscilla seemed to have become assistants and fellow helpers of the apostle Paul. Acts 18:18: "After awhile, Paul tarried there in Corinth and then he took his leave. He

sailed from there into Syria and with him Priscilla and Aquila."
Verse 19: "He came to Ephesus and left them there." Now,
watch. Paul went on his way, but he left Aquila and Priscilla in
Ephesus. Do you notice that already in one chapter, this is the
second move they've made? They have moved from Italy to Corinth; now from Corinth to Ephesus. On the move constantly. But
every time they moved, they used that move as an opportunity
to establish people in Christ.

In the city of Ephesus they began evangelistic activity, talking
to people, helping in the work of Jesus. When Paul returned to
Ephesus in chapter 19, there was a city ripe for harvest. Why?
Because there was a dedicated Christian household there using
its home as an outpost of witness. It was a concerned household.

The church at Ephesus had a visiting preacher to come by.
This is recorded in verse 24. Tune in on this. This will be a blessing to mature Christians. In Acts 18:24, a young preacher
named Apollos came there. Apollos was a preacher's preacher.
He was eloquent, golden-tongued. "He could preach the stars
down." And "he was mighty in the Scriptures." The power of
God was on him as he taught and preached the Word.

Verse 25: "He was instructed in the way of the Lord. He was
fervent in spirit." Where I came from, you would call him a fire-
ball. His preaching was electrifying. I love to see a person who
believes what he believes enough to become excited about it,
stirred up about it. I don't like these Milquetoast, namby-pamby,
pussy-footing preachers.

Did you hear about the wimp of a preacher who said, "If you
don't repent (so to speak) you'll go to hell (as it were)." I'm not
too wild about that.

I like a man to be bold and tell it like it is. Apollos was eloquent, mighty in the Scriptures, instructed in the things of the Lord, and fervent in spirit. And yet read the rest of verse 25, and you will discover that he was still somewhat deficient in the Word. Evidently, Aquila and Priscilla were deep in the things of God. They seemed to be tremendously well-read in the Scriptures and able to teach them. And so, when young Apollos came, for all of his zeal, for all of his eloquence, for all of his fire, he was not really able to feed Aquila and Priscilla. He was on a lower level of spiritual maturity.

What were they going to do? Let me tell you what they didn't do. OK? They didn't start criticizing the young preacher; they didn't start visiting other churches; they didn't start showing their displeasure and expressing their disgruntled spirit. By the way, if you are a mature Christian and a faithful student of the Bible— and have been for several years—could I give you a word of warning? One of the dangers of spiritual maturity is that you will become filled with spiritual pride and become a spiritual snob— and you might come to the point that you are so mature, so deep in the Word that no man of God can feed you anymore. That happens all along. I hear people remark, "Well, you know, I'm not getting fed." Some of the puffed-up people who use that old bit of "I'm not getting fed," have begun to prosper, and now they have come to the point they don't really want to pay the price to be a soul-winning, on-fire Christian for the Lord. So, what do they want? They want to go where they can sit back and get fed with the Word, and never ever get on the firing line for the Lord. You never come to the point that you can't get a blessing out of the simplest, humblest child of God if you have an open heart to get it. I listen to guys on the radio sometimes. I have heard preachers who spray the first three rows when they open their mouths. They have to keep their windshield wipers running. I've heard men murder the King's English, and yet they blessed me.

If you have an open heart, and he's a true man of God, you can always get fed from a man of God. If you want to garner a blessing, you always can.

No, they didn't become critical. They didn't show their displeasure. They didn't run off somewhere else where they could "get fed." Could I paraphrase verse 26. It says, that when Aquila and Priscilla heard him, "they took him aside and expounded unto him the word of God more perfectly." Maybe this is what happened. One Sunday morning after the service, Aquila came up to Apollos and said, "Brother Apollos, we'd like to invite you over to our house for dinner today. Sister Priscilla's cooking a splendid feast." And, Apollos accepted. They had a wonderful meal together, and after the meal they were sitting around together. Humbly, sweetly, and lovingly, they shared with the young preacher what God had given to them.

Folks, do you know anything in the Word of God that somebody else doesn't know? The Bible says, "What dost thou have that thou didst not receive?" Anything you know about the Bible that some other people don't know is not any reason for you to become spiritually haughty and arrogant. It's a reason for you to be humble and to sweetly and lovingly share it with others. The Sunday School teachers in our church are terrific. They bless me, and I learn from them. Every child of God is a priest before God. He has the right to study the Bible under the leadership of the Spirit Himself, and if God shows him something that some other Christian doesn't know, he should share the bounty. So this couple instructed that young preacher in the things of the Lord. Guess what happened to him? He became so superlative that a bigger church in Corinth called him to be their pastor, and they lost him! *A concerned household!* It was *a Christian household,* it was *a concerned household,* and it was . . .

A Church Household

I want to show that to you in 1 Corinthians 16. In 1 Corinthians 16:19: "The churches of Asia salute you. Aquila and Priscilla salute you much in the Lord with the church that is in their house." Did you know it was the late second or early third century AD before there were any church buildings? The church of the Lord was in the house. Everywhere Aquila and Priscilla went, they had a church in their house. They won people to the Lord; they organized them into a church.

Maybe they met in the workshop out back or in the "den." I don't know, but there was a church in their house. There was the simplicity of it all. They didn't have a lot of things we have today, but they had the things we have that really matter. They had the Son of God, the Spirit of God, the Father, and the Word of God. They enjoyed the fellowship of the children of God, and wherever you have those ingredients, you have a church. We must never forget the simplicity of it all. Buildings are useful, and thank God for them; they enable us to congregate people. But buildings do not have to be elaborate monuments. They are just places where people can gather together to study the Word of God. You can worship Jesus Christ knee-deep in carpet or on sawdust floors—it really doesn't matter.

And so everywhere they went, they were soul-winners, having a church in their house. Is there a church in your house? Have you gathered people together in your family, and is it a household matter? We have all kinds of sweet children. Do you see this pretty little boy I'm holding? Every Sunday, Shane is here. Shane Hammonds, two years, ten months old. I get to see him about every Sunday night. His daddy is, I believe, a truck driver. His daddy has been saved about six months, and every time the doors open, that new Christian father has little Shane in the house of God. You know, that's exactly what God wants in your house. He wants your house to be a church household where the family comes to the house of God, learns about the Lord, and is encouraged to live for Jesus.

10
A Storm in the Middle of God's Will

Ill that God blesses is our good,
And unblest good is ill;
And all is right that seems most wrong,
If it be His dear will!
                    —Frederick William Faber

Acts 27:18-25

And we being exceedingly tossed with a tempest, the next day they lightened the ship;

And the third day, we cast out with our own hands the tackling of the ship.

And when neither sun nor stars in many days appeared, and no small tempest lay on us, all hope that we should be saved was then taken away.

But after a long abstinence Paul stood forth in the midst of them, and said, Sirs, ye should have hearkened unto me, and not have loosed from Crete, and to have gained this harm and loss.

And now I exhort you to be of good cheer; for there shall be no loss of any man's life among you, but of the ship.

For there stood by me this night the angel of God, whose I am, and whom I serve,

Saying, Fear not, Paul; thou must be brought before Caesar: and, lo, God hath given thee all them that sail with thee.

Wherefore, sirs, be of good cheer: for I believe God, that it shall be even as it was told me.

Acts chapter 27 presents the voyage of Paul en route to imprisonment in Rome. Back in Acts 22, Paul became a prisoner. From that point on to the conclusion of Acts, Paul is not free. Acts 27 tells us how God brought him to the place where he would be able to give his testimony before Caesar himself.

As you read these verses of Scripture, you may become aware of the fact that this is a very detailed account of ancient seafaring, a gem of literary skill. It is a classic. It is a unique chapter in all the Word of God.

I do not know this to be a fact, but I have heard that the midshipmen at the Naval Academy in Annapolis are required to read this chapter because there is no other piece of literature that gives as much detail about ancient seamanship. This chapter, interestingly enough, has been used through the years as a case for the accuracy and reliability of the Word of God. This chapter has been a bulwark in establishing the historicity of Acts.

Decades ago, a group of agnostics decided they were going to destroy the Bible. They were going to do this by attacking the historical statements in the New Testament. The scoffing scholars divided among themselves different portions of the New Testament to study and thus prove its historical facts to be incorrect. A scholar, Sir William Ramsey, was chosen to investigate the Book of Acts. His purpose was to prove that the historical references in the book were inaccurate. After meticulous analysis and study, Ramsey came to the conclusion that rather than being historically inaccurate, the Book of Acts was amazingly accurate and reliable.

In fact, he came to believe that the Bible is indeed the inspired, infallible Word of God. This chapter, as uninteresting as it might seem to you, was instrumental through the Spirit of God in bringing Ramsey to faith in Jesus Christ. His writings at that time stood as some of the greatest defenses of the reliability of the New Testament ever written. We must keep in mind that the accuracy of this chapter helps undergird our confidence in the total inerrancy of the Word of God.

By the way, the Bible never has to fear honest, thorough scholarship and investigation. The Book will always stand the test. If you come to the Bible with an attitude of believing faith, if you are willing to be shown the truth by the Spirit of God, the Bible will always come out absolutely pure, absolutely infallible.

When you read this chapter, you will notice that you have high adventure on the high seas—a story of seafaring, of storm, and of shipwreck, an account of danger and deliverance. Many storms are recorded in the Bible. Do you remember the storm in the Book of Jonah? (Jon. 1). Jonah was told by God to preach the truth in Nineveh. Jonah didn't want to obey God, so he decided he would go in the opposite direction. He boarded a ship because he had the idea one could sail away from God. Then the Lord hurled a storm onto the sea. If you want to sail into the biggest storm of your life, just run from God's will for your life. You may find yourself in a belly of a great fish as you cry out to God for deliverance. You cannot escape God.

But Paul's storm was an altogether different storm. Jonah was in a storm outside the will of God. Paul is in a storm right in the middle of the will of God.

Sometimes we have the idea that if we're in the will of God, there will be no difficulties or problems in life. This chapter reminds us that a person can be dead center in the will of God and sail right into the eye of a storm. And other storms are mentioned in the Bible.

Do you remember the storm in Mark 4:35-41? The Lord Jesus was on a boat with the disciples on the Sea of Galilee. Jesus was asleep down in the stern. Then there arose a tempestuous gale on the sea, not unusual on the Sea of Galilee. Galilee was in a basin surrounded by mountains. When the cool air whipping down from the mountains would collide with the hot air coming from Galilee, sudden storms were the common result. The disciples were afraid that they were not going to survive, yelling, "Master, we perish!" They shook him and moaned, "Don't You care if we die?" Have you ever been in a storm and asked, "Lord, I'm going under. Don't you care?" Of course, we do know that Jesus cares. Does Jesus care? "I know He cares. His heart is touched with my grief. When the days grow weary and the long nights dreary, I know my Savior cares." So Jesus looked out over the stormy waves and he spoke: "Peace, be still." *The New American Standard* Bible puts it: "Hush, be still." I like that. And the waves lay down at the feet of Jesus like obedient puppies. Jesus Christ is not only Lord of the land but also Lord of the sea.

But now this is a different sea altogether. That was a storm when the Lord of the servants was on board. Here is a storm when the servant of the Lord is on board. I feel that the storm, the sea, and the voyage are used as an illustration of the voyage of life. Do you remember in 1 Timothy 1:19 where Paul wrote about a group of people who had made shipwreck of the faith? He uses the figure of the voyage to describe life. And do you remember in 2 Timothy 4:6 that Paul was coming down to the conclusion of his life and he testified, "The time of my departure is at hand." And the word "departure" is actually a nautical term, taken straight from seafaring terminology. Paul was saying, "It's time for me to pull up anchor and set sail on the sea of eternity, and one of these days I am going to land on the shores of glory." Life is compared to a voyage on the sea. There is a danger in using allegory to teach the Bible. If you're not careful, you can go too far. Here I am using allegory because I believe I have Bible precedent for it. I want to use Paul's experience on the sea and the shipwreck of the ship as an allegory of the voyage of life. There is an old hymn we used to sing, "Jesus, Savior, pilot me, over life's tempestuous sea." When you peruse this voyage of Paul and compare it to the voyage of life, there are three observations I want to make about it. First, I want to consider . . .

The Winds of Providence

Let us discuss the winds of providence. You will notice in verse 4: "And when we had launched from thence, we sailed under Cyprus because the winds were contrary." Reference is made to winds several times in this chapter. Verse 13 he talks about the south wind blowing softly. In verse 14, "But not long after there arose against it a tempestuous wind, called Euroclydon" [or a "Noreasterner"]. It reminds us of the winds of providence in life.

As God's people we believe there is the providence of God at work in the circumstances of our lives. The same God who controls the wind is the One who controls the circumstances of our lives. Sometimes there are cool, refreshing winds. At other times there are stormy, cold winds—different circumstances, same providence of God behind them all.

Think for a moment about the *winds of difficulty*. Sometimes you find yourself in a storm. All kinds of storms blow in life's voyage—a storm of sickness, a storm of failure, where your self-confidence is shaken, and in a storm you feel helplessness. You're not sure how the situation is going to turn out. You're in a storm of difficulty. Sometimes the storms assume the form of unexpected tragedies. I remember several years ago in Georgia, there was a fine young pastor of a rural church in Howard County. I remember the dreadfully rainy day when the roads were slick. I was out driving in it. That Godly pastor's wife and three babies were out in the weather trying to reach home. As the car came to an intersection, the young wife put on her brakes, but the brakes didn't hold. She ran through the intersection, a car hit her, and she and the three babies were instantly killed. The preacher found himself in a storm of tragedy that would be enough to sink many a vessel in life. I remember attending the funeral and will never forget that young preacher as he stood before the casket of his own wife and his three offspring. In the midst of the storm of a tragedy like that, he gave a positive testimony to the sustaining grace of Christ amid a tragedy of life.

How do you respond when the storms come into your life? Anybody can live for the Lord when it's smooth sailing. What do you
do when the winds of misfortune beat against you? The important fact in life is not that storms come. The Bible says the rain
falls on the just and the unjust. It's not a matter of if storms are
going to come—the question is not if they come but how are you
going to respond when those storms beat on you? How you respond to the storms will speak volumes about how successful
you are in the voyage of life. Even in the storms of difficulty, God
is behind the scenes. Never judge God's heart or judge God's
hands. Never judge what you see happening. You and I have
only the underside of the picture.

I remember hearing the story about a mining town in the Brit-
ish Isles where there had been a tragedy. Many miners had lost
their lives in a mining accident. And as the pastor of the local
church stood before grief-stricken people that day, he held up a
bookmark. All they could see were tangled threads that made no
sense whatever—different colors, different sizes absolutely tangled together, nothing intelligible to them. Then he took the
bookmark, and he turned it around. On the other side the
threads had been embroidered into the words "God is Love."
Regardless of what comes in life, there is one constant you
always need to remember—God is love. Never judge God's hand
apart from His heart.

And so the voyage of life has its *winds of difficulties*—its *winds
of danger*. But then, praise God, the voyage of life also has its
winds of delight. Sometimes the delightful winds blow. Life is not
all tragedy. There are days of delight and days of joy. I am thankful for the delights that God permits to enter our lives—the joy of
a family, the joy of a baby, the joy of the fireside. There is nothing

in this world as sweet and as precious as the hug of a little child. Many a man comes home at the end of the day about ready to give up, but a little child runs to dad, jumps up in his arms, and says, "Hi, Dad!" And all the cares, all the heartaches, and all the failures of the day are evaporated in the words of a child. I thank God when the sweet winds of family blow. The little things in life. In the morning, one of the reasons I believe in the resurrection is because I experience one every morning of my life. My wife Janet is just the opposite. She is up at the crack of dawn. Now, I arise very early in the morning, but I don't do it because I want to. I do it because I have to and because I need to, and I am so sluggish in the morning. In this voyage of life, it's not all storms. There are some calm waters along the way. And we ought to be thankful for little things. The voyage of life not only has its *winds of difficulty* and its winds of delight, but the voyage of life also has its *winds of deliverance*. Sometimes the Lord sends that wind of deliverance in His providence, in His sovereign purpose for your life. God sends deliverance. So the voyage of life has its *winds of providence,* but now there's a second factor about the voyage of life—

The Anchors of Promise

In verse 29 they were fearing that they might run aground upon the rocks, and so they cast four anchors out of the stern and wished for daybreak. We know the purpose of an anchor. An anchor is to keep the ship steady, providing security for the ship and keeping it from drifting. An anchor. In the voyage of life you need some anchors to hold you down—to give stability and security in your life. They have nothing they can hold onto, nothing solid; they're tossed to and fro. Whenever the winds come, they're blown away. Ephesians 4:14 admonishes us that we no longer be children "carried about by every wind of doctrine." Lost people are like a ship without an anchor. They have no stability, nothing that is authoritative in their lives.

Paul's ship had four anchors that gave them security in their voyage. Let me suggest four anchors for the voyage of life, four great promises that can anchor you and give you a sense of stability. Anchor number one I call *the throne of God*.

In Psalm 45:6, the Bible says, "Thy throne, oh, God, is for ever and ever." God is still on His throne. God has not abdicated His throne. "Have faith in God. He's on His throne. Have faith in God. He watches o'er His own. He cannot fail—he must prevail! Have faith, have faith, in God!" The throne of the eternal God is an anchor you can hold onto when the storms of life are raging all around you.

Anchor number two I call *God's church*. God's church is like an anchor. Jesus declared, "Upon this rock I will build my church, and the gates of hell shall not prevail against it" (Matt. 16:18). God's church is an anchor on which you can build your life. I feel sorry for people who don't have a church they can turn to in times of tragedy. A few years ago I was asked to conduct a funeral for a family in our community, and they had no church relationship. And so I asked them, "Why did you ask me to do this funeral? As far as I know, you don't attend any church. I'm honored that you asked me to do the funeral. I was just curious." I will never forget their answer: "No, Preacher, we don't have a church, but where can you turn to except the church in an hour like this?" Every person needs a local church. When the storms come, it will bless you to have a Sunday School class that will help you make it through that time. When the storms of bereavement, heartache, and tragedy almost capsize your boat, it helps to have a fellowship of believers who care and understand. I have an anchor, my local church. I would also suggest the anchor of *God's precious Word*. First Peter 1:25 says, "The Word of the Lord endureth for ever." It is what one calls the impregnable rock of Holy Scripture. There is an equilibrium and security noticeable in the life of a person who reads and obeys the teachings of the Bible. A nation shipwrecks when it departs from the anchor of Holy Scripture. A church shipwrecks when it avoids or turns away from the anchor of Holy Scripture. A life can do nothing but run aground when it turns away from the anchor of Holy Scripture. Anchors of promise. God's throne is forever. God's church is unassailable. God's word endures forever.

Now I give you a fourth anchor. The fourth anchor you need is *God's hope*. Hebrews 6:19-20 assures us: "Which hope we have as an anchor of the soul, both sure and stedfast, and which entereth into that within the veil whither the forerunner is for us entered even Jesus, made an high priest for ever after the order of Melchisedec." We have an anchor for the soul, sure and steadfast, and the writer says that it has entered into that within the veil. The picture here is graphic, pregnant with meaning. Right before the entrance to the harbor, there was usually a sandbar. And the sandbar impeded the ship from going into the harbor. The only time the ship could get into the harbor was when the tide came in, and the water level rose to the point that the ship could navigate over the sandbar.

Sometimes the ship would reach the harbor before the tide came in. So the sailors would throw the anchor into the harbor. The ship wasn't in the harbor yet, but the anchor was there. They were waiting for the tide to come in. At times the wind would blow that old ship. But the seamen knew they were secure. Their anchor was already in the harbor. They merely had to wait until the tide came in. If you're a child of God, you have an anchor for the soul. And that anchor is none other than the Lord Jesus Himself. And Jesus, your anchor, has already gone into the harbor. He is already at the right hand of the Father. And let the storms assault and the winds beat on the old ship of life. That's all right. One of these days when the tide goes in, we're going in because we're already anchored in Christ Jesus.

Life's voyage has some *winds of providence*. It has some *anchors of promise,* and then it has . . .

The Boards of Protection

Follow my train of thought most carefully. In the text, after the ship had been on this voyage for a period of time, the ship was in danger of being dashed on the rocks. The apostle Paul stood before them and gave them a word of encouragement almost like the Lord Jesus used. Verse 22: "I exhort you, be of good cheer." Doesn't that sound like the Lord Jesus? And then Paul shared with them the vision he had the night before and the promise that God had given to him for them. What was the promise in verse 22? "For there shall be no loss of any man's life among you, but of the ship." Now pay attention to verse 24: "Fear not, [Paul, quoting the Lord, said,] Thou must be brought before Caesar and lo, God hath given thee all them that sail with thee. Wherefore, Sirs, be of good cheer, I believe God. It shall be even as it was told me." It was a promise of protection. God said, "Paul, I'm going to give you everybody on this ship. You're not going to lose a one." The ship wrecked and broke apart on the rocks. Before the shipwreck verse 34 said, "Wherefore I pray you to take some meat. For this is for your health. For there shall not a hair fall from the head of any of you." Paul reaffirmed God's promise. "God is going to keep His promise. He's going to protect you. You're going to be all right. Listen, sometimes in life's voyage it looks as if everything is going to pieces, as though your whole world has exploded around you. What happened to them? Verse 44: "And the rest some on boards and some on broken pieces of the ship, and so it came to pass that they escaped all safe to land." The men aboard were tossed out into the ocean. One by one Paul and all those aboard grabbed the boards and flotsam and jetsam which floated by. And the next thing you know, they're all holding onto boards. Boards of protection. Exactly what God said He would do, He did, and they all came to shore protected by the promise and the power of God. And bless your heart, I have good news for you. You may come in on a board. You may come in barely holding onto something, but you have a God in heaven who has committed Himself to care for you. You are under the protective power of God, secure in the Lord Jesus Christ. The devil can't get you. He can't rob you of your salvation. The moment you receive Jesus Christ as your Savior, you are just as good as in heaven as if you've been there 10,000 years. God gives protection in the voyage of life. We have come to the end of the voyage; now let me ask you a question. How are you doing in life's voyage on the sea of life?

When I was a boy, I saw a well-known picture. You probably have seen it, too: a picture of a young man standing at the helm of a ship. Behind him in the picture, looking over his shoulder, is the Lord Himself. And the point of the picture is my message. If you're going to make the voyage of life successfully, you must be sure that Jesus is on board your vessel. Is Jesus the pilot of your life's vessel? Have you invited Jesus on board your life? The Lord has arranged the circumstances of your life to bring you to salvation. And you know what I'm going to invite you to do? Receive Jesus as your Savior and Lord.